WILDLIFE

AN ENFORCEMI

Vivek Menon
Ashok Kumar

Second Updated Edition

Natraj Publishers
Dehra Dun

in Collaboration with

WILDLIFE PROTECTION SOCIETY OF INDIA
New Delhi

Produced by WILDLIFE PROTECTION SOCIETY OF INDIA
M-52, Greater Kailash, Part - I, New Delhi - 110 048

First published, 1998.
Second updated edition 1999.

Published by Natraj Publishers, 17, Rajpur Road, Dehradun.

© 1998 Wildlife Protection Society of India
ISBN 81-85019-83-5

Citation: Menon V. and Kumar A. (1998), Wildlife Crime: An Enforcement Guide, Wildlife Protection Society of India, New Delhi.

Vivek Menon,
Executive Director, Wildlife Trust of India,
Senior Technical Consultant, Asian Elephant Conservation Centre &
Hon. Wildlife Warden, Delhi, PO Box 3150, New Delhi-110003.

Ashok Kumar,
Trustee, Wildlife Trust of India, New Delhi

Illustration and layout : A.V. Prasanth

Cartographer : Virender Kumar

Cover photo : Vivek Menon

The designations of geographical entities in this publication and the presentation of the material do not imply the expression of any opinion whatsoever on the part of the authors or Wildlife Protection Society of India concerning the legal status of any country, territory or area, or of its authorities, or concerning the delimitation of its frontiers or boundaries.

Other publications by the Wildlife Protection Society of India include:
• *Handbook of Environment, Forest and Wildlife Protection Laws in India*, 1997 in collaboration with Natraj Publishers.
• *Fashioned for Extinction : An Expose of the Shahtoosh Trade - 2nd edition 1998*
• *India's Tiger Poaching Crisis*, 4th Edition, 1998

In collaboration with Asian Elephant Conservation Centre
• *A God in Distress: Threats of Poaching and the Ivory Trade to the Asian Elephant in India,* 1997
• Signed & Sealed - The fate of the Asian Elephant, 1998

WPSI audio-visuals include:
• *Bones of Contention*, 1996
• *Birds of the Indian Monsoon*, video release - 1997

Printed By Print Style, New Delhi

Acknowledgements

An enforcement guide of this nature cannot be produced without a number of people helping out. Those who wrote the original material that has been used as reference are perhaps the most to be thanked. We would also wish to thank the following persons who helped this project more directly in one way or another.

Ms. Belinda Wright, Executive Director, Wildlife Protection Society of India made valuable contribution to the text, technical inputs and layout, Brij Bhushan Sharma, Sanjay Upadhyay, Baiju Sanyal and Bindia Sahgal helped with many of the references and drafts. A.V. Prasanth, the illustrator and designer for the project had to spend many days tearing up fresh layouts as ideas were scrapped overnight. Ranga Nathan helped in print and production. At the computer, P. T. Suresh, Sathyan A.V. and Abdul Gaffar were invaluable. We are thankful to them. Ravi Singh, an old friend and editor, and V.K. Karthika helped in the copy-editing and proofing of the text.

John Sellar from the CITES Secretariat, S. K. Mukherjee and S.P.Goyal from the Wildlife Institute of India, Pradeep Srivastava, Deputy Commissioner, Delhi Police and Jean Paul Luquet of the French Customs helped in providing inputs for various sections. George Schaller, that amazing pioneer of wildlife studies, once again has generously lent his photos of the Tibetan antelope. The section on law has been framed by Mr. Raj Panjwani, Advocate.

For the second edition we are thankful to Dr. Ed Espinoza, Dr. Bonnie Yates, Dr. Cookie Sims & Dr. Jo Ann Schafer of the US Fish & Wildlife Service, Forensic Laboratory for their comments and and Mr. K.S.N. Chikkerur DIG (Police) Karnataka for valuable inputs. We also thank Ritu Singh and Preeti Singh, WPSI for editorial assistance.

The publication of this book has been financially supported by Save the Tiger Fund, a special project of the National Fish and Wildlife Foundation created in partnership with Exxon corporation.

To all of these people our heartfelt thanks.

Foreword

Government of India
Ministry of Environment &
Forests,
Paryavaran Bhawan
CGO Complex, Lodi Road,
New Delhi-110003

*I*t is heartening to note that the Wildlife Protection Society of India is bringing out an Enforcement Guide on Wildlife Crime.

During recent years, there has been a lot of concern about the heavy toll on wild animals being taken by the poachers and persons involved in illegal trade. The state governments are now convinced that their efforts need to be augmented by the wildlife enthusiasts outside the government system. With this objective in mind, a large number of Honorary Wildlife Wardens have been appointed across the country. The publication would serve as a useful document for educating the Honorary Wildlife Wardens and other enforcement officials about the relevant laws and identification of species in trade. I, therefore, compliment the Wildlife Protection Society of India for the initiative taken by it. I am sure the long association of the authors with control of illegal wildlife trade in the country would give the publication the inputs that are crucial for effective protection of wild animals.

I wish the Wildlife Protection Society of India as well as the authors of the book all success.

(S.C. Sharma)
Addl. Inspector General of Forests
and
CITES Management Authority of India

Contents 6

Acknowledgements	3
Foreword	5
Introduction	9
What is wildlife crime?	10
Why stop wildlife crime?	12
How large is wildlife crime?	13
Who can stop wildlife crime?	14
Which laws regulate wildlife crime?	15
What is CITES?	16
How does CITES work?	17
CITES permit check	18
Legal procurement certificate	20
Export consignment check	21
Methods of smuggling	22
Special smuggling techniques	24
Data storage system	25
Methods of poaching	26
Anti-poaching checklist	28
Patrolling	29
Gun discipline	30
Informants	31
Intelligence network	32
Undercover operation	34
Surveillance	36
Crime scene search	37
Collection of evidence from crime scene	38
Conducting a criminal investigation	40
Interrogation techniques	41
Using metal detectors	42
Detecting time of death	43
Identification of teeth and claws	44
Differentiating wounds in carcasses	46
Post-mortem	47
How to go to court	49
Disposal of confiscated specimens	52

General identification tips	53
Bear bile	54
Musk	55
Ivory	57
Rhino horn	59
Tiger and leopard parts	61
Fur	64
Shahtoosh	67
Reptile skin	69
Live reptiles	72
Live mammals	73
Live birds	75
Turtles	77
Frogs leg	79
Swiftlet's nest	80
Coral	81
Butterflies	83
Antlers	84
Medicinal plants	85
Ornamental plants	87
Timber	89
Ornamental fish and shell trade	90
Feathers	91
Others	92
Fakes	93
Annexure-I : Handling of live reptiles	95
Annexure-II : Plants banned for export	96
Annexure-III : Identification of bear bile	97
Annexure-IV : Identification of antlers	99
Annexure-V : Identification of horns	100
Annexure-VI : Identification of ivory	101
Annexure-VII: Eco-message format	103
Contact addresses	105
Notes	108
Photo credits	109

Introduction

*A*lthough wildlife conservation in India dates back more than two thousand years, the fact that India plays an important role in the trade in wild animals and plants was not generally known till even ten years ago. India is an importer, exporter and a conduit for wildlife that enters the $ 25 billion annual global trade. In response to this, the Government of India has set its policy tone and made its laws quite unambiguously. Most wild animals in India are protected and it is a crime to kill any of them, with the exception of rats, mice, crows and fruit bats. Many plants are also protected by law. Export and import of all wild animals and their parts and products (including shed peacock feathers, that was once permitted) is prohibited and the same is true for more than forty species of plants. India was one of the earliest members of the Convention on International Trade in Endangered Species of Wild Fauna and Flora (CITES), thereby pledging international support to an ideal. Both in its domestic and international policy on wildlife, India has retained the strong conservation ethics that are part of the country's history and tradition.

Despite all these laws and policies the illegal trade in wildlife continues to flourish. Just as mere laws do not bring down the incidence of heinous crimes in society, the poaching of animals, uprooting of plants and their subsequent trade also has to be dealt with in the field. We firmly believe that the time has come to recognise the gravity of the situation and to try and arrest the cataclysmic decline of species. This guide is meant to help enforcement personnel, who are concerned with controlling this trade, in carrying out their duties.

To make this an easy exercise we have illustrated the book generously and kept written text to a minimum. The book is divided into five broad sections that group subject matter. While the first section of the book contains introductory material that gives an overview of wildlife trade, the last contains appendices, lists of useful addresses and notes for further reference. In between are three sections on law enforcement techniques, species overview and identification, and legal and policy matters. As identification is the most difficult part, this section is given in colour.

The guide is meant for Honorary Wildlife Wardens, staff of forest and wildlife departments, customs, coastguard, police, paramilitary (Border Security Force, Indo-Tibetan Border Police, and the Central Reserve Police Force), Directorate of Revenue Intelligence, Central Bureau of Investigation (including the cell of Interpol), Railway Protection Force, Foreign Post Office, and, indeed, any other person dealing with this subject. It should also encourage these different departments to collaborate with each other and develop a common aim to stamp out this trade.

It is hoped that the book will be a practical guide to on-field implementation and that it will contribute to controlling the second largest illegal occupation in the world: wildlife crime.

What is wildlife crime?

*W*hat is wildlife crime? What actually constitutes wildlife? How serious is the issue that we are dealing with? A basic understanding of these parameters is necessary before a more detailed examination is made of enforcement. The basics can be addressed in five points.

Orchid

Fish

Tiger

Butterfly

1. Wildlife

The Wildlife (Protection) Act, 1972 defines wildlife as "any animal, bees, butter-flies, crustacea, fish and moths, and aquatic or land vegetation". There is a popular misconception that "wildlife" refers only to mammals and birds or, according to some, only to large mammals. On the contrary, the definition embraces all life forms that are wild.

2. The offence

Wildlife crime is contravening any domestic or international law concerning wildlife, be it by poaching for food or fun or by killing to supply an illegal wildlife trade or by possessing illegal material or smuggling it across borders. In India, killing most species of wildlife is a crime. If it feeds into a large, illegal global racket, it is also a crime contravening international treaties and law. Poaching and smuggling wildlife must be given the priority that other heinous crimes are accorded.

Food

Sport

Trade

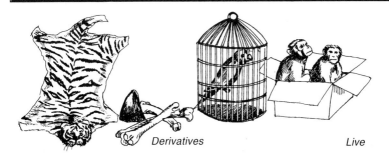

Derivatives   *Live*

3. Commodities in the trade

Wildlife trade can be in live animals or their parts, products and derivatives, including plant extracts and parts of animals used in medicines. In fact, live animals form only a small part of the trade.

4. Levels of the trade

Wildlife trade can be at the local village level, regional retail and wholesale levels or international import and export levels. A wildlife criminal may therefore be a villager or a wealthy international smuggler. These distinctions are important while enforcing the law as the latter often get away at the expense of the former.

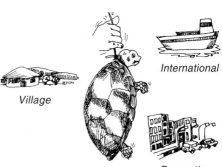

International

Village

Domestic

5. Value of the trade

The global value of wildlife trade as given by international enforcement agencies is second only to narcotics in the illegal arena. Wildlife crime is therefore the second largest illegal occupation in the world.

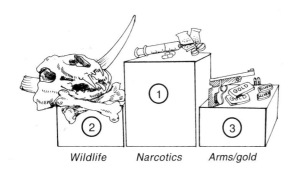

Wildlife   Narcotics   Arms/gold

Why stop wildlife crime?

Wildlife crime must be prevented because:

➤ Species such as the passenger pigeon, West Indian monk seal, great auk and Steller's sea cow have already become extinct because of demands from the wildlife trade.[1]

➤ Others like rhino, elephant, tiger, giant otter, Spix's macaw and the Orinoco crocodile are on the brink of extinction.

➤ Although habitat loss or degradation is a major worry in the fight against species extinction, wildlife crime works at the cutting edge for a species. Any increase in poaching can have a huge impact on populations.

➤ Wild plants that provide genetic variation for crops and are the natural source of many medicines are threatened by the trade.

➤ Any wildlife commodity that is used, such as timber, fish, plants (almost all over the world) and animal species (in some parts of the world), is a natural resource that should not be over-exploited.

➤ Illegal wildlife trade is part of the general crime syndicate of any country, including drugs, gun-running etc., that must be eradicated.

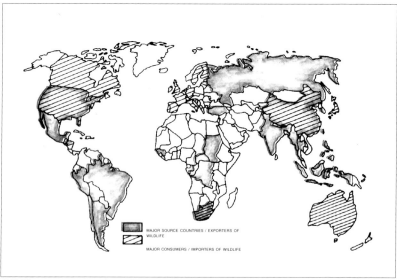

Wildlife consumer and producer countries

Numbers in global trade[1]

Record global prices

Monkeys — 25-30,000

Trained falcon — upto US $ 10,000

Live birds — 2-5 million

Rare parrot — upto US $ 40,000

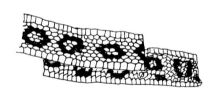

Reptile skin — 10 million

Rare butterfly — upto US $ 30,000

Orchids — 10 million

Rare orchid — upto US $ 2000

Important: Prices are indicative of how large the illegal trade is and how important it is to stop it. Every specimen or derivative will not fetch these prices.

*E*nforcement of laws against wildlife crime in India is complicated by the fact that a large number of agencies are directly or indirectly involved in trying to stop it. Given the complex system that exists, it is extremely important that agencies co-ordinate with each other and work in a co-operative fashion to tackle wildlife crime. The agencies listed below are connected with stopping wildlife crime and therefore are also potential users of this guide.

Anti-poaching agencies

- ❑ State Wildlife Departments.
- ❑ State Forest Departments.
- ❑ Ministry of Environment and Forests.
- ❑ Army (wherever applicable).
- ❑ Police.
- ❑ Indo-Tibetan Border Police.
- ❑ Border Security Force.
- ❑ Coastguard.

Anti-smuggling agencies

- ❑ Customs.
- ❑ Wildlife Protection Department (GOI).
- ❑ Railway Protection Force.
- ❑ Directorate of Revenue Intelligence.
- ❑ Foreign Post Office.
- ❑ Central Bureau of Investigation
- ❑ Interpol Unit of CBI.
- ❑ Police.
- ❑ Border Security Force.
- ❑ Indo-Tibetan Border Police.

Support agencies

- ❑ Wildlife Institute of India.
- ❑ Central and Regional Forensic laboratories.
- ❑ Zoological Survey of India.
- ❑ Botanical Survey of India.
- ❑ Central Marine Fisheries Research Institute.

- ❑ Honorary Wildlife Wardens and Special Police Officers.
- ❑ Wildlife Protection Society of India.
- ❑ Wildlife Trust of India.
- ❑ Regional NGOs.
- ❑ TRAFFIC-India.

Which laws regulate wildlife crime?

*I*ndia controls wildlife crime through three primary legislations: the Wildlife (Protection) Act, 1972; the Customs Act, 1962; and the Export-Import Policy. Apart from this, a few other Acts are also used. Some salient features of these Acts are listed below.

Wildlife (Protection) Act, 1972

❑ Applicable all over India except Jammu and Kashmir which has its own Act.

❑ Prohibits hunting of any wild animal listed in any of its schedules except mice, rats, common crow and fruit bats.

❑ Schedules I,II,III and IV list different protected species, the killing or trade of which are punishable by varying penalties. A Schedule I offence can earn a repeat offender 6 years in prison and a fine of Rs 25,000. Section 51 lays down penalties for violations of the Act.

❑ Schedule V lists vermin which may be killed. Schedule VI lists protected plants.

❑ The Act also sets down the rules of a protected area and penalties for violating them.

Foreign Trade (Development and Regulation) Act, 1992

❑ The Export-Import Policy is framed under this Act. It lists prohibited and restricted items.

❑ This Act replaces the earlier Imports and Exports (Control) Act, 1947.

❑ Wild animals including their parts and products such as ivory are prohibited for import.

❑ Wild animals and their derivatives are prohibited for export. Wood and certain wood products are also prohibited or regulated.

❑ 29 plant species are prohibited for export. Others are restricted and need a licence.

Customs Act, 1962

❑ All offences against CITES (see page 16) and the Export-Import Policy are punishable under the Customs Act.

Other Acts

❑ The Indian Penal Code, 1860.

❑ The Code of Criminal Procedure, 1974.

❑ The Prevention of Cruelty to Animals Act, 1960.

❑ The Arms Act, 1959.

What is CITES?

CITES or the Convention on International Trade in Endangered Species of Wild Flora and Fauna is the treaty that monitors and regulates international trade in endangered species. It came into force in 1973 and today 145 countries are signatories to it.

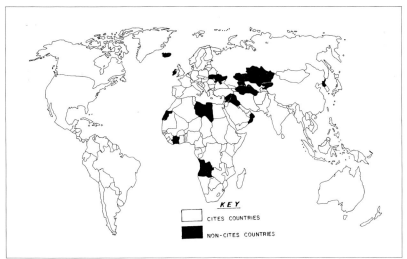

Member countries of CITES

CITES is the largest international conservation treaty. It functions in the following manner:[2]

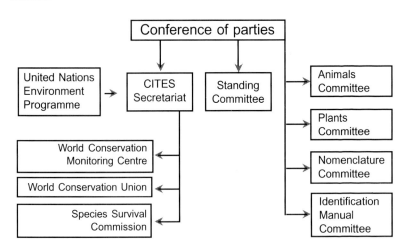

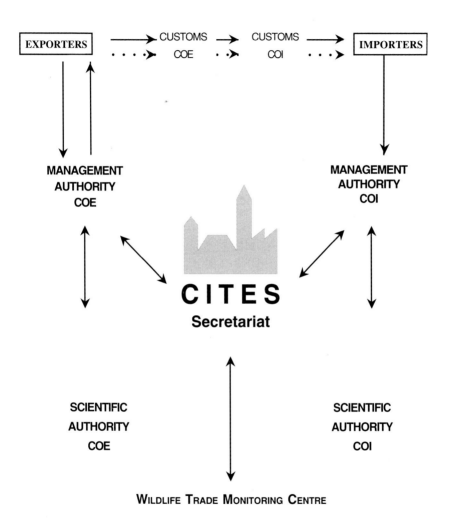

EXPORTERS → CUSTOMS → CUSTOMS → IMPORTERS
COE · ·> COI · · ·>

MANAGEMENT AUTHORITY COE

MANAGEMENT AUTHORITY COI

CITES
Secretariat

SCIENTIFIC AUTHORITY COE

SCIENTIFIC AUTHORITY COI

WILDLIFE TRADE MONITORING CENTRE

KEY²

——— Export Permit
· · · CITES Merchandise
COE   Country of Export
COI   Country of Import

*T*he permit must be for the particular shipment.[2]

1. The species on the document must be the species being exported.

2. The product being traded must be from the species mentioned.

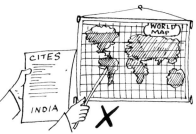

3. The quantity being traded should not be more than the quantity mentioned in the document.

4. The source of the animal should be the same as mentioned in the document.

5. If tags or marks are mentioned in the document, they must be on the specimen in an untampered condition.

The CITES permit is compulsory for international trade in any species in Appendix I, II or III of the Convention.[3]

1. The permit must be original and authentic.

2. It should have no modification or alteration unless with the signature and stamp of the CITES Management Authority.

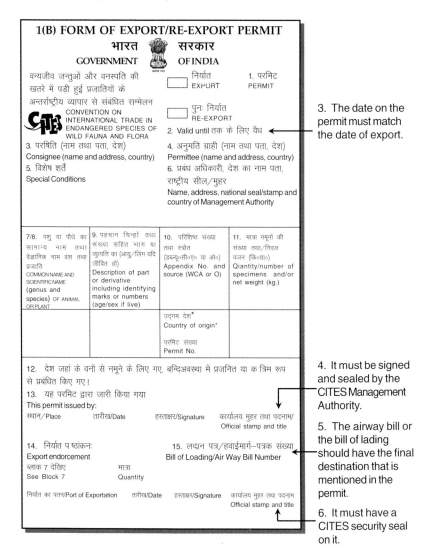

1(B) FORM OF EXPORT/RE-EXPORT PERMIT

भारत सरकार
GOVERNMENT OF INDIA

वन्यजीव जन्तुओं और वनस्पति की
खतरे में पड़ी हुई प्रजातियों के
अन्तर्राष्ट्रीय व्यापार से संबंधित सम्मेलन

CONVENTION ON
INTERNATIONAL TRADE IN
ENDANGERED SPECIES OF
WILD FAUNA AND FLORA

निर्यात
EXPORT

पुनः निर्यात
RE-EXPORT

1. परमिट
PERMIT

2. Valid until तक के लिए वैध

3. परिषति (नाम तथा पता, देश)
Consignee (name and address, country)

5. विशेष शर्तें
Special Conditions

4. अनुमति ग्राही (नाम तथा पता, देश)
Permittee (name and address, country)

6. प्रबंध अधिकारी, देश का नाम पता,
राष्ट्रीय सील/मुहर
Name, address, national seal/stamp and
country of Management Authority

7/8. पशु या पौधे का सामान्य नाम तथा वैज्ञानिक नाम वंश तथा प्रजाति COMMON NAME AND SCIENTIFIC NAME (genus and species) OF ANIMAL OR PLANT	9. पहचान चिन्हों तथा संख्या सहित भाग या व्युत्पति का (आयु/लिंग यदि जीवित हों) Description of part or derivative including identifying marks or numbers (age/sex if live)	10. परिशिष्ट संख्या तथा स्रोत (डब्ल्यू०सी०ए० या ओ०) Appendix No. and source (WCA or O)	11. मात्रा नमूनों की संख्या तथा/निवल वजन (कि०ग्रा०) Qiantity/number of specimens and/or net weight (kg.)
		उद्गम देश* Country of origin* परमिट संख्या Permit No.	

12. देश जहां के वनों से नमूने के लिए गए, बन्दिअवस्था में प्रजनित या क त्रिम रूप से प्रबंधित किए गए।

13. यह परमिट द्वारा जारी किया गया
This permit issued by:

स्थान/Place   तारीख/Date   हस्ताक्षर/Signature   कार्यालय मुहर तथा पदनाम/Official stamp and title

14. निर्यात प ष्ठांकनः
Export endorsement
ब्लाक 7 देखिए
See Block 7

मात्रा
Quantity

15. लदान पत्र/हवाईमार्ग—पत्रक संख्या
Bill of Loading/Air Way Bill Number

निर्यात का पतन/Port of Exportation   तारीख/Date   हस्ताक्षर/Signature   कार्यालय मुहर तथा पदनाम Official stamp and title

3. The date on the permit must match the date of export.

4. It must be signed and sealed by the CITES Management Authority.

5. The airway bill or the bill of lading should have the final destination that is mentioned in the permit.

6. It must have a CITES security seal on it.

Legal procurement certificate

A legal procurement certificate (LPC) is a document issued by the state forest departments that certifies that the commodity in question has been lawfully obtained by the possessor. Given below is a sample of a legal procurement certificate issued by a state forest department.

(SPECIMEN)

LEGAL PROCUREMENT CERTIFICATE

(FAUNA/FLORA/DERIVATIVES)

SPECIES OF WILD FAUNA AND FLORA

CERTIFICATE NO. __________

VALID UPTO: ____________

Details of earlier LPC(s) Cancelled:

(No. and date, issued by ______________)

1. This Certificate is hereby issued in favour of ________________ ________________________________holder of Licence No. _____ for Manufacturing and dealing in trophies/uncured trophies in terms of Wild Life (Protection) Act, 1972, for the local Trade of parts/ derivatives from Fauna and Flora as detailed below.
2. I hereby certify that the parts/derivatives from fauna/flora as detailed below of which Local Trade is permitted was procured in the Wild.

Description of Item (also state the scientific name)	Common Name	Quantity/ No. of Packages,	Weight Nett. Kgs.	Weight Gross Kgs.	Identification Mark, on the packages
1	2	3	4		5
Shed Antler of Chital *(Axis axis)*	Chital	10 Bags (Ten Bags)	Kgs. 1000	Kgs. 1200	Seal

Date of Issue ______________

Signature/Designation

of the Sealing Officer

Sold to:

____

____

____

Chief Conservator of Forests

(WL) cum-Chief Wild Life Warden.

The following points are a sequential check of a consignment to be exported. Enforcement officers must necessarily take into consideration all the following points before clearing export.

1.	Specimen in hand for export	
2.	If domestic species	Check quarantine regulations (also legal procurement certificate for plants)
3.	If wild species	Check designated port of export
4.	If not being exported from Mumbai, Calcutta, Chennai and Delhi for animals and Kochi for plants	Export refused or possible forfeiture or seizure
5.	If yes, check if prohibited under Wildlife (Protection) Act and Import-Export Policy	
6.	If yes	Export refused or possible forfeiture or seizure
7.	If not, check if it is a CITES listed species	
8.	If not	Export cleared
9.	If yes, check CITES Appendix	
10.	If Appendix-I, check if consignment is commercial	
11.	If yes	Export refused or possible forfeiture or seizure
12.	If no, check CITES Certificate and Export permit	
13.	If not okay	Export refused or possible forfeiture or seizure
14.	If okay check Legal Procurement and No Objection Certificate	
15.	If not okay	Export refused or possible forfeiture or seizure
16.	If okay, check consignment	
17.	If not okay,	Export refused or possible forfeiture or seizure
18.	If okay	Export cleared
19.	If Appendix-II/III, check CITES certificate and Export permit and proceed as from point 12.	
20.	Notify Regional Deputy Director Wildlife Preservation at points 5 and 7.	

Methods of smuggling

*T*he common *modus operandi* used by wildlife smugglers can be summarised as under:[3]

1. **Concealment:** Concealing or hiding a contraband item is the most common method of smuggling. Examples are, using false-bottom briefcases, body-belts or pouches, putting reptiles inside socks etc. There are also cases where the item is simply put into the baggage hoping that there is no enforcement check.

2. **Misdeclaration:** This can happen in three ways:

   a) Misdeclaring a species: Peacock chicks can be labelled as domestic hen chicks, frogs leg as chicken legs, ivory carvings as cattle bone, etc.

   b) Misdeclaring numbers: Items where a certain quantum is allowed for export, such as peacock-feathers can be taken out in larger volumes by misdeclaring.

   c) Misdeclaring value: This is an excise problem but under-invoicing is a very common trade fraud. Today this is common only with a few species.

3. **Forgery of permit:** Normally done at the stage of import as officials would be unused to the permits of the exporting countries. LPCs and CITES certificates are often forged.

Jha

4. **False 'captive-bred' or 'cultivated' claim:** Exporters often claim that an animal or plant is not wild at all and provide LPCs which are forged.

5. **Re-export laundering:** When ivory, reptile skins etc. were allowed to be imported into India to be crafted and then re-exported, items of Indian origin were often added. This is difficult to regulate as wastage while crafting cannot be easily quantified.

6. **Laundering legal stocks:** Some wildlife products are legally traded in Jammu and Kashmir. Fur from other states, for example, is smuggled into Jammu and Kashmir and thus legalised.

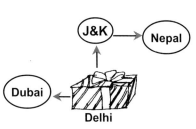

7. **Using safe countries:** The prime example is Dubai and nearby ports into which the wildlife items are smuggled using established smuggling routes. Once there, they re-emerge as legal stock.

8. **Trade adulteration or faking:** This is primarily to cheat the customer. Musk, bear bile, etc., are adulterated with such items as bee's wax and honey. Fake rhino horns, fur, etc. are also common. (see chapter on Fakes).

Important: Law-enforcement information exchange systems should be used to alert other agencies of any new *modus operandi*. This is vital for a quick reaction to new developments.

Sometimes wildlife smugglers use special techniques. Two techniques currently in use are: involving diplomats in smuggling (thereby gaining diplomatic immunity) and mailing small items as post and courier parcels.

Wildlife crime and diplomats

- Diplomatic immunity that is granted to foreign diplomats and members of missions is sometimes violated. Diplomats are rarely checked at border points.
- Smuggling by diplomatic channels has in the past involved rhino horn, ivory, tiger products, and many other forms of wildlife.
- Diplomats can smuggle items in their personal effects while flying or while driving across borders in their CD-plated cars. They may even poach and carry poached animals with them.

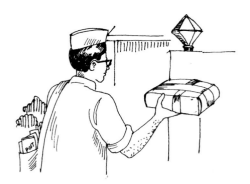

Wildlife crime and the mail

- Mailing wildlife items has become a common smuggling technique. Foreign post office personnel, in particular, have to act as supplementary wildlife enforcement officers and should be trained in checking consignments.
- Common wildlife items smuggled by post are reptile skins, furs, bristles and hair, shahtoosh, feathers and sometimes even ivory and musk pods.
- Packages should be searched or, at the very least, X-rayed.
- In some places sniffer dogs are used to detect wildlife products. This is an efficient technique.
- Intelligence gathering is useful in identifying persons using postal or courier services.

*D*ata can be stored in either old-fashioned paper files or in state-of-the-art computer systems. The most important rules to follow while doing so are:

Accuracy
Cross-check all information before entry, update periodically, give credibility rating to information.

Cross-referencing
Pull out key words and attributes and cross-reference wherever applicable. Link different databases if feasible.

Security
Ensure physical and electronic security. Maintain back-ups at a different location.

Ease in retrieving
Make system user-friendly. Base it on the most frequent form of analysis.

A sample data entry format is shown for poaching and seizure offences.

Structure of Mortality Database for Elephants

CASE NO .... N OF REC ....
(Nature of record; S-Seizure, D-death)

DAY .... MONTH .... YEAR ....

PERSON .... ADDRESS ....
(Person (s) involved)

LOCATION .... AREA CITY .... STATE ....
(Location of the Event)

DETECTION .... SOURCE ....

REMARKS ....

SEX................ AGE .... N OF MORT ....
(Nature of Mortality; poaching/natural/accidental, etc.)

HEIGHT .... LTUSK LEN .... LTUSK GIRT ....
(left tusk length)   (left tusk girth)

RTUSK LEN .... RTUSK GIRT .... CIR F ....
(right tusk length)   (right tusk girth)   (Circumference front foot)

CIR H .... QTY KG .... QTY ITEM ....
(Circumference hind foot)   (quantify kg. if seizure) (quantity item if seizure)

QTY TUSK .... TOLL ....
(quanity tusk if seizure)   (no. of elephant death)

Structure of Accused Database

CASE NO .... NAME .... DESCRIPTION ....
(Poacher/trader, etc)

ADDRESS ....AREA.....................

STATE .... PHONE .... SOURCE ....

REMARKS ....

*T*here are a large number of methods used by poachers to trap or kill animals. This is dependent on the species which is to be caught and the final market. The following illustrations depict some of the more common methods. It is important to remember that these change continuously and enforcement agencies must always be on the look out for new methods being used by poachers.

Pit poaching (for rhinos, large mammals)

Electrocution (for rhinos, tiger, elephants, wild boar, etc.)

Shooting (all kinds of mammals, some birds)

Poisoning (large herbivores, big cats)

Trap and snare (mammals, some reptiles)

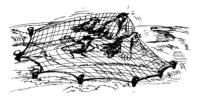

Net (small birds, small mammals, butterflies)

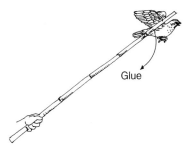

Stick and glue (fast-flying birds)

Taking young from nest-holes (birds)

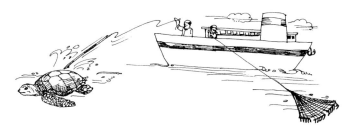

Harpooning (whales, turtles)

Trawling (corals, shells, marine invertebrates)

Digging for underground animals (snakes, lizards porcupine etc.)

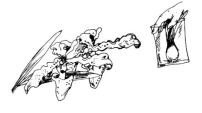

Collecting plants from the wild

Important: Each area will have its own regional variations. These pages only illustrate common methods used by poachers. A poacher in need will improvise. A flexible approach is the key to anti-poaching.

Anti-poaching checklist

A park manager who is in charge of the security of an area must be prepared for anti-poaching operations at all times. If poaching is already rampant, immediate steps must be taken to curb it. The following checklist comprises basic questions that should be addressed in order to put an anti-poaching plan into operation. If the answer to any of the questions is Yes, go to the next point. If No, then tackle the problem and then proceed.

1. **Is an anti-poaching plan in place ?**
Prepare an anti-poaching plan on the lines of a working plan.

2. **Do you have enough men to effectively patrol the area?**
Fill sanctioned posts, lobby for more posts, consider daily-wage personnel, consider Point 12.

3. **Is the motivation level high enough for maximum effectiveness?**
Provide basic amenities to staff and plan specific morale building exercises. Request NGOs and HWLWS to help.

4. **Are the staff trained in all aspects of anti-poaching and follow-up ?**
Train staff in arms handling, ambush and counter-ambush, interrogation, undercover operations, identification of species, and litigation.

5. **Are the staff well armed?**
Requisition for adequate arms and ammunition. Work out annual replacement schedules.

6. **Is the existing communication system adequate?**
Check layout and maintenance of fixed and mobile units. Request NGOs and donor agencies for help.

7. **Are vehicle numbers sufficient?**
Check number, maintenance and appropriateness. Request NGOs and donor agencies for help.

8. **Are staff acquainted with terrain?**
Shift patrolling duties so that every staff member is acquainted with entire terrain.

9. **Is an intelligence network in place?**
Establish a network. Consult pages 32-35.

10. **Is the area regularly patrolled?**
Set up patrol parties. Consult page 29.

11. **Is the flow of funds to the lowest level smoothandtimely?**
Work out system to ensure timely fund flow.

12. **Are the local villagers being used in anti-poaching ?**
Hold village meetings, consider setting up village patrols, consult your Honorary Wildlife Warden.

13. **Is the media on your side?**
Cultivate media at regional and national level by feeding them news and talking to them.

14. **Are the local police stations, customs unit, army unit helping you?**
Cultivate officers in charge and request specific help. Offer the assistance of your agencies wherever possible.

15. **Are the local magistrates and courts sympathetic?**
Utilise the services of NGOs to make courts and magistrates aware.

16. **Do you have good links with NGOs?**
Cultivate local, regional and national NGOs and work with them.

*O*nce you have gone through the anti-poaching checklist, more specific measures need to be taken to ensure that individual components of the anti-poaching scheme are carried out in a well-planned manner.

A suggested patrol plan

1. A patrolling plan must be drawn up by each range officer on a monthly basis or on a pre-decided frequency.
2. Plot the plan onto a topographical sheet of the area.
3. The plan can follow the demarcations of a range, section and beat, with the range officer, forester and specified forest guard in charge of each area.
4. Patrolling paths should ideally be plotted in a random manner. In areas where this is not possible, paths already made by man or animal (e.g. a rhino *dandi*) may be used.
5. Patrolling paths must be varied regularly. This may be based on a random choice to maximise coverage, or based specifically on intelligence reports.
6. Ideally, patrolling should be done by a team of 4-5 people. A minimum of three persons per patrol is necessary for effective challenge in case of an encounter.
7. If manpower is insufficient, reduce number of patrols and shift paths more frequently. Do not reduce number of persons in a patrol party.
8. The patrol path must be plotted so that communication with nearby check posts, guard huts or the main headquarters is possible at any given time. Ideally, walkie-talkies must be provided to each team.
9. If this is not possible, plan the location of anti-poaching huts or check posts so that patrol parties are always within a couple of kilometres from a check point. This is essential in areas where exit points for poachers are within the same distance. In case of interior areas, communication equipment is essential.
10. Train patrolling parties in camouflage, ambush, counter-ambush etc., and keep them in good physical condition. Arms training must be regularly refreshed and practised.
11. Daily patrol findings must be logged in a patrol book kept at the beat office. This must be submitted to the range office at regular intervals decided by the range officer.
12. Patrol findings must be analysed to plan new patrol routes and strategies.
13. Rotate patrol parties at regular intervals.
14. Remember that staff incentives are an important motivating factor. If formal incentives are not forthcoming, plan informal motivational tactics.
15. Liaise with local villagers during a patrol to gain information and their confidence.

Important: Patrolling is the most effective physical deterrent to poaching. Patrolling must be done in conjunction with intelligence gathering to achieve best results. Patrolling should ideally be done on foot or bicycles as it is a silent method and covers all sorts of terrain.

*U*nless a firearm is in proper working condition and maintained so that it is ready for use at any given time, it's use diminishes. The following instructions are basic law enforcement guidelines meant for any kind of firearm.

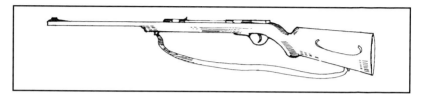

Caution is the best principle

1. Never forget that even the safest weapon can be dangerous to you and others if not handled correctly. Before handling any weapon, thoroughly familiarise yourself with its functions and handling procedures by carefully reading the instruction manual.
2. Always handle an unloaded weapon as if it were loaded.
3. Keep your finger off the trigger until you actually wish to fire the gun.
4. Whether loaded or unloaded, do not point the weapon at anyone. The barrel should always face the ground or the sky when not in use. Always hand over a gun with the butt facing the recepient.
5. Never use force when using, cleaning or assembling a weapon.
6. Only weapons in perfect working order are safe to use.
7. Always have your firearm inspected by a qualified gunsmith if it has suffered from corrosion, other external damage or if it has been dropped.

Care of firearms

1. A monthly maintenance drill is essential for proper upkeep of the firearm.
2. Before going out on patrol, wipe the barrel out with a dry flannel cloth.
3. After firing, clean the barrel thoroughly with a flannel cloth, then apply a thin film of 'Singer machine oil' to the bore. Lubricate the action slightly.
4. During periods of high humidity keep the gun dry by wiping it frequently to avoid rusting. Apply thin layer of lubricant as waterproofing.
5. Wipe again with a rod-flannel if oil is applied inside the barrel.
6. Always keep a screwdriver, flannels (*chindi*) and gun oil at hand.
7. Inspect barrel for mud deposition. Check fit of barrel into butt to avoid misfires, backfires or bursts.
8. Do not drag the firearm in the mud while on patrol. The gun should always be on the shoulder and should never be used to clear obstacles.

Important: Practice makes perfect. If ammunition is available, practice target shooting. Forest departments may wish to link up with other enforcement agencies for training. Make sure that supplies of ammunition are timely and that stocks are always maintained.

Informants

*T*he use of informants is a key component of any intelligence system. If used well, informants can determine the final result of an investigation. Developing an informant, using his information and keeping the informant over a number of years is a vital skill.

Who can be an informant?
1. Any person is a potential source of information.
2. Law enforcement personnel outside your agency.
3. An associate of the suspect, present or past.

How do you categorise informants?
1. Confidential informants: Persons wishing to remain anonymous for various reasons.
2. Public informants: People who have no reservations about being identified as the source of information.
3. Special employees: Persons who are full-time informants working with your agency.

When to use an informant?
1. To conduct surveillance in areas where a law enforcement person cannot go undetected.
2. To gather information from sources not readily available to law enforcement officers.
3. To conduct controlled undercover negotiations.
4. To testify for the government at legal proceedings.

What motivates an informant?
1. Fear
2. Revenge
3. Money
4. Personal Ego
5. Perversion
6. Repentance
7. Social commitment

How does one develop an informer ?
1. Treat each and every person as a potential informant.
2. Understand the motivating factor for the informant and fulfill it.
3. Reassure the informant of the amount of protection that can be given. Do not make promise difficult to keep. Be honest.
4. Meet informant frequently at safe places. Maintain good rapport and trust.
5. Corroborate information given by informant and assign a credibility rating to the informant.
6. Be truthful and fair in all dealings with the informant.
7. Ensure protection of your informant. A person will give information only if he feels safe.

How does one categorise information from an informant ?
1. Document all dealings with informants immediately.
2. Assign a code name or number to the informant for use in all documents.
3. Create and maintain secure files with photos, fingerprints, record checks and biographical data.
4. Document date, time, place, witness, and subject of all contacts with informants.
5. Cross-reference information either with databases or manually.

Important: The protection of an informant's identity is a professional and ethical obligation. Informants are used not only to help solve a crime but also to gain intelligence that can prevent it.

*S*etting up a system of information gathering, analysis and evaluation is the most important facet in anti-poaching or anti-smuggling. The procedure for setting up an intelligence network is as follows:

1. Collection

➢ The collection of information must be carefully planned, co-ordinated, and directed against a specific target, or gaps in information. It must be reviewed at different stages of the process.

➢ Overt collection of information can be through investigators, law enforcement agency records and from other sources.

➢ Covert collection of information can be through physical or electronic surveillance, informants or undercover agents.

➢ Collection of data must be done in accordance with the laws of the land.

2. Evaluation

➢ All information must be verified by an independent source if possible.

➢ Credibility ratings must be given to each item of information.

➢ Decide on the leads to be followed up.

3. Collation

➢ A filing system with cross-referencing and cross-indexing should be set up.

➢ A coding system for this should be worked out with emphasis on quick recovery of data.

➢ Useless and incorrect information should be sifted out.

4. Analysis

➢ An analyst must re-assemble the investigators' data.

➢ Preliminary hypotheses from this must be reviewed.

➢ Close contact must be maintained between analyst and investigator, if seperate.

➢ The analyst must keep in mind the final use of the analyses and proceed based on that.

5. Reporting

➢ Can be oral or written but tailored to the need of the recipient.

➢ Should be objective, logical, concise and on the basis of accurate information.

➢ Should separate hypotheses from facts.

6. Dissemination

➢ Intelligence report must go through a one-person command (head of unit).

➢ List of recipients, depending on security clearance, should be prepared.

➢ Confidentiality of report is important but should not be the decisive factor in dissemination.

7. Re-evaluation

➢ Constantly review operation.

➢ Evaluate quality of reports, collection system, analyses.

➢ Request feedback from users of intelligence system.

➢ Develop tests to measure the ability of system to do quick analysis.

➢ Change the system of information gathering or analysis based on the re-evaluation.

The following points should be kept in mind while running an intelligence network:

Location
➢ The network should be headquartered at a place where the transfer of information to the recipient agencies is easy.
➢ The security of the location is paramount.

Staff
➢ The network should preferably be run by a small, efficient autonomous unit.
➢ Integrity,capability and personality are crucial in all staff.
➢ Investigators must be experienced, motivated, capable of taking initiative and of interpreting factual accuracy.
➢ Analysts must be intelligent, logical and precise.
➢ Specialist analysts should be used for certain skills such as legal issues, identification, etc.
➢ There should be one head of the unit with complete responsibility.

Training
➢ The value of good observers and good reporters should be made clear.
➢ The complexity and sophistication of organised crime must be emphasised.
➢ The goals of the unit must be made clear.
➢ Basic training in identification of species and products should be given.
➢ Use of the intelligence gathered, methodology of collection and analysis, new developments in collection techniques, court matters etc., must be explained.

Security
➢ Background investigation should be conducted on every new unit member. Periodic updates must be undertaken.
➢ Entry to the intelligence area should be restricted.
➢ Files and computers must be physically and electronically protected. Duplicates must be maintained at two locations.
➢ Phone lines, computer lines and all means of communication should be checked at periodic intervals.
➢ Security is not an end in itself. It should not be used to conceal mistakes, corrupt activities, etc.

Potential sources of information
1. Informants (see page 31).
2. Crime scene investigation (see pages 37-39).
3. Documents (judicial, official, contracts, deeds, certificates, letters, books, memos etc).
4. Business and service agencies (banks, hotels, tax agencies, telephone, credit, insurance, etc).
5. Law enforcement agencies (records of offences, arrests, court proceedings, investigative reports, gun registrations, fingerprints, traffic accidents etc.).
6. General publications (newspapers, magazines, telephone and business directories, etc.).
7. Surveillance (see page 36).

Undercover operation

*A*n undercover operation is legal, covert, investigative work which involves deception of, and association with, the suspect. This is often the only technique that can be used against well-organised criminal elements.

Planning

1. Establish reliability of intelligence and review background information to determine objectives.
2. Collect background information on the activities, habits, records and vices of suspects; area of operation, ethnic background, language and even style of dress.
3. Evaluate manpower required including informants, law enforcement officers, follow-up team and back-up team.
4. Evaluate equipment including vehicles, cameras, video and audio equipment, communication equipment and weapons.
5. Estimate expenses for manpower, equipment running, subsistence, lodging, emergency money and 'show money' (where appropriate).
6. Establish criteria for calling off operation.

Initiation

1. Continue to develop background on suspects and maintain surveillance.
2. Select and test equipment including vehicles,communication equipment, tapes, cameras, etc.
3. Select undercover agent who is willing, even-tempered, adaptable, technically sound, patient and has initiative. Specifically, the agent should have appropriate physical appearance, know the local language and fit into the required role.
4. Develop background story which should accommodate actual background of agent as much as possible.

5. When selecting assumed identity try to choose one with similar personality traits and personal background.
6. When choosing a name, try and retain first name or nickname. Change last name.
7. Provide as much documentation as possible to the agent that corroborates his background story.
8. Establish means of communication including contact persons.
9. Brief all participants in the operation.

Operation

1. Approach suspect. If possible, use informer for introduction to save time, effort and money.
2. This can be a problem if there is a double-crosser, or if the informer is difficult to control. In which case try and approach suspect directly, pretending that it is a chance encounter or by using a lure.
3. Gain confidence of suspect. Use identification material that suspect can see. Speak only of things that the informer is confident about. Always bargain with suspect. Use false role even when not in front of suspect.
4. Maintain surveillance at site, prior to, and after, meeting suspect.
5. After returning to safe area, scrutinise evidence and record statements.
6. Conduct supporting investigations if necessary. Liaise with other agencies.
7. Evaluate progress.

Termination

The operation should be terminated if:
1. Investigation is complete.
2. Cover is blown.
3. No results are forthcoming nor forseeable.
4. There is imminent danger to agent.

Evaluation

Identify and evaluate success and problems.

Be careful of:
1. Faulty equipment such as audio and video recording systems.
2. Personal agenda of informants.
3. Entrapment by informer or suspect.

Investigation tools

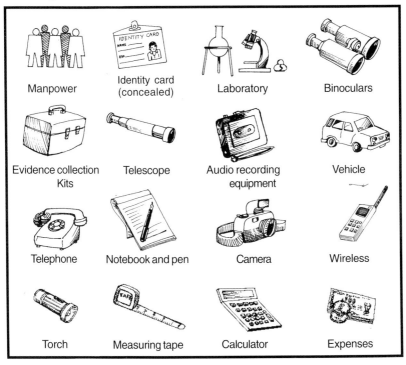

Manpower	Identity card (concealed)	Laboratory	Binoculars
Evidence collection Kits	Telescope	Audio recording equipment	Vehicle
Telephone	Notebook and pen	Camera	Wireless
Torch	Measuring tape	Calculator	Expenses

Important: The physical well being of the agent and the informer is more important than a day's operation. **Withdraw if risky**. Continue later. Stay within legal bounds. Do not pay cash advances for goods or place orders for future delivery. This will be counter-productive to wildlife conservation for obvious reasons.

Surveillance

Surveillance, covert or overt, is used to obtain intelligence or evidence in a crime for a possible cause for arrest or search warrant, or to provide protection to undercover operators. Surveillants must be alert, natural, patient, resouceful and have good endurance skills.

Types of surveillance

Vehicle
Use at least two vehicles. If possible rotate lead vehicle. Turn off door-operated lights.

Foot
Ideal in most conditions. Use at least two to three persons.

Boat or aerial
If the terrain so demands.

Stationary or stake-out
Ideal in areas where prior information exists.

Surveillance techniques
➢ Use observation posts that offer perfect concealment or are obviously overt such as roadside vendor, telephone repair, etc.
➢ If camouflaging post, do so at the rear as well.
➢ Stalk in and stalk out. Slow movement is essential. Freeze if detection is imminent, do not duck.
➢ Avoid leaving footprints and stepping on dry leaves or twigs. Paths to post must be surveyed beforehand.
➢ Allow at least 30 minutes in low light conditions for the eye to adjust.
➢ Check communication systems beforehand. Have spare batteries for equipment.
➢ Always make contingency plans.
➢ Avoid deodorants, colognes etc. Do not carry reflective objects, metal or plastic objects that are not secured (to avoid noise), unnecessary food, drink or equipment.
➢ Be patient. Keep alert by keeping mind occupied.

*I*f a wildlife crime has been committed, an important starting point to the investigation is searching for evidence at the scene of the crime. The following steps are recommended.

1. Isolate scene with rope or tape.
2. Keep written notes or audio recordings.
3. Take photos (and video if possible).
4. Sketch area and positioning.
5. Search for evidence (see below).

6. Take footprints of animals and humans in the area (see page 38).
7. Collect evidence (see page 38).
8. Search for wounds or marks on the animal.

How to search for evidence[4]:
The eye has to be trained to pick up evidence. Use one of the methods given below to maximise efficiency.

1. Start searching point-to-point in a straight line.
2. Divide area into quadrants. Search one quadrant at a time.
3. Cover the area in a spiral manner.
4. Send your men from point to point and then back again.
5. Send your men in a radial manner from the centre of a supposed circle.

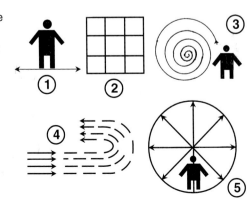

Collection of evidence from crime scene

Collecting evidence from the scene of a crime has to be done in a scientific and precise manner in order for the evidence to have some use in the final investigation. The following evidence is commonly available at a poaching site.[4]

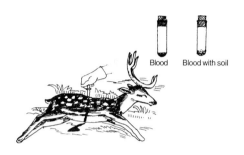

Blood
➤ Collect blood from animal's body using a dropper into a test tube. Seal it tight with a cork.
➤ If blood is found on soil, collect blood with soil in a test tube and seal it.
➤ Collect soil without blood from the scene.

Footprint/pugmark
➤ Photograph print before taking impression.
➤ Put glass on the print. Sketch from above.
➤ Your eyes must be at 90° to the print in order to avoid parallax error.
➤ Fill print with Plaster of Paris. Allow it to dry. Collect the cast.

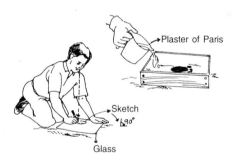

Hair
➤ Use forceps to collect hair for evidence.
➤ Do not bend hair while collecting.
➤ Collect hair from the root if possible.
➤ Place in a plastic bag (not paper envelope). Seal and label it.

Firearms
➢ Use gloves to pick up the firearms.
➢ Do not insert any object into the barrel of the gun.
➢ Note position of lock, hammer and catch (if present on the firearm) and do not change it.
➢ Note if gun has been fired or not.

Fingerprint
➢ Photograph fingerprints before lifting them.
➢ If fingerprint tape is available use it to collect print.

Bullet
➢ Take out bullet from animal's body without scratching it. Place it in a paper bag, seal it and label it.
➢ Cartridge cases found outside should also be collected in paper bags, sealed and labelled.
➢ In case bullet is embedded in hard object (eg. tree), cut around the bullet and place the whole block in a paper bag. Seal it and label it.

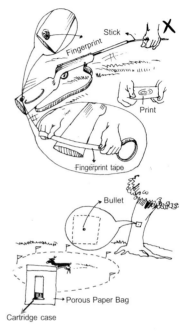

Photograph
➢ A photograph is useful evidence. On it should be date, time, place of incident, brief description, name & signature of photographer. Always place a case no. or some other identifier in each picture alongwith ruler or something that references size.

Things that can go wrong[4]

1. Failure to recognise what is evidence.
2. Too many bystanders - improper protection of the crime scene.
3. Too many officers - contamination of evidence.
4. Using hit-or-miss type search techniques.
5. Lack of organisation and communication in the search.
6. Failure to search outside the immediate crime scene.
7. Failure to search area for witnesses.
8. Failure to take proper notes, photograph or video etc.
9. Contaminating the evidence by handling.
10. Placing wet/stained items in plastic bag before drying.
11. Packing more than one item in the same package.
12. Bad collection of fingerprints.
13. Jumping to conclusions and making the scene fit theories.
14. Failure to restrict information.

Conducting a criminal investigation

*O*nce the evidence on the scene of the crime is collected, the next step is to conduct a criminal investigation into the crime. Remember that for an investigation to start, a crime need not have been committed and this could be the beginning of an effort to foil the crime. For simplicity you can divide the investigation into five phases.[4]

1. Intelligence gathering
➢ Try and identify the suspects.
➢ Through various sources, determine the scope of activity of the suspects.
➢ Document and validate all the intelligence information gathered.
➢ Analyse the intelligence reports. Please consult pages 32 and 33 for   this phase.

2. Decision to conduct the investigation
➢ The final decision to conduct the investigation must be taken after the background intelligence has been analysed. At this stage, you can decide to close the case if background information so indicates.

3. Planning the investigation
➢ Is there sufficient manpower?
➢ Who will supervise the investigation?
➢ Who will co-ordinate the investigation and serve as the "team leader"?
➢ How many investigators/officers are available to provide for surveillance, evidence analysis, technical support?
➢ Is the equipment available adequate and well maintained?
➢ Are there arrangements for the storage of evidence?

4. Implementing the plan
Always remember to:
➢ Stay flexible.
➢ Continue to update your intelligence.
➢ Continue to identify your defendants, suspects, and charges.
➢ Gather, label, analyse, evaluate and secure your evidence.
➢ If needed, obtain and execute arrest warrants, summons, search warrants.
➢ Conduct interrogations, take confessions in presence of two independent witnesses.
➢ Produce in court within 24 hours.
➢ Release synopsis of the investigation to the media.
➢ Prepare and submit your evidence. Brief lawyer.

5. Evaluate your results
➢ Ask yourself what finally was accomplished. Evaluate if investigation has been a deterrent to future illegal activities and if, due to the case, more update and accurate intelligence is available.

A suspect may have to be interrogated before and or after the crime. In many cases interrogation of suspects may help prevent the crime. In case the crime has already been committed, interrogation becomes an investigative tool to help bring the criminals to justice. The following points may be followed or adopted during interrogation.[5]

1. Questioning should usually be done by more than one person.
2. A brief check on the suspect's background must be made before interrogation.
3. Make use of available investigation reports, including from other enforcement agencies, to brief interrogator before the session. The interrogator must know more about the case, or pretend to know more, than the suspect.
4. Cross-question suspect on details of the crime to detect contradictions.
5. Ask questions, even if they are not relevant to the interrogation, that allow you to be one-up on the suspect. This could generate a fear psychosis in the suspect's mind.
6. The suspect should be made aware of the conviction laws and the rigorous penalties he has to face if proven guilty by a court, and the possible repercussion to his family.
7. When appropriate, use the blow-hot blow-cold technique, whereby one investigating officer pretends to be tough and merciless while the other pretends to be more understanding. In many cases the suspect succumbs to this tactic.
8. If two persons are caught they should first be interrogated separately and then, if necessary, together.

9. If wildlife products are seized, effort should be made to find out where the goods originated, names of accomplices and names of ultimate buyers. Leads should be followed up immediately and swiftly to recover more articles and arrest accomplices.
10. In poaching cases or attempted poaching, names of other gang members, financiers, *modus operandi* of poaching, ultimate buyer of poached article, are vital to obtain. Try to obtain information that can be used to prevent further poaching in the area, not just investigate the current case.
11. Try to use independent witnesses during questioning. If not possible they must be present during recording confessions. Do not use your own staff as witnesses.
12. Confessions made in an enforcement office may not be admitted by a court, but are still important for the purpose of investigation. However, Section 50, subsection (8) & (9) of WPA are relevant in case of wildlife offences.

Important: No technique is uniformly effective on all suspects. Be flexible and use intuition and initiative to question the suspect depending on the case in question.

*A*mong new techniques used in solving wildlife crime, the relatively old human forensic and crime-solving technique of using metal detectors is rapidly gaining popularity and is now established as an essential tool.

Metal detectors should be used to scan carcasses for bullets and also for finding evidences from the scene of a crime.

Locating and removing pellets using X-Ray is often difficult as X-Ray machines are not available in the field and it is difficult to obtain two-dimensional projections. Models of metal detectors such as Whites Electronic Model 4900/D (modified with a hand wand) is very useful in the field. The entire carcass should be scanned with the hand wand in a systematic and regular manner.

For recovery of spent bullets from a scene of crime the following steps are useful:

1. Establish point of firing
2. Test aim from point of firing into target location and therefore establish the search area for bullet streak marks.
3. A good metal detector picks up a 40 grain bullet within 10 cm or a 150 grain bullet within 25 cm.
4. See if the bullet streak marks that you find are indicating a bullet stoppage or a deflection. Remember that each deflection slows a bullet down.
5. If only streak marks are found at the site, by aiming back from the streak marks, the appropriate firing point can be calculated.

It is important to note that although metal detectors look very simple to use, they should only be used after prior familiarisation and practice on known specimens to ensure accurate results.

The examiner must make sure that his hands and person are metal free including of rings, keys, watches etc.

It is important to use a control sample of lead and steel pellets to calibrate the unit before the test is done on the carcass. Note that if a steel and lead pellet are in close proximity, metal detectors will detect both as steel.

Gunpowder Residue Test

Whenever an offender is apprehended with revolvers, rifles, pistols or muzzle loaders in the process of poaching it is important to subject both the left and the right hand of the accused to a test. This test which is called the gunpowder residue test is very simple and can be done anywhere. The only materials are:

1. A clean wad of cotton-wool (available in medical stores)
2. Distilled water (also available in medical shops)

Method of taking hand-wash

1. Dip sufficient quantity of clean cotton wool into distilled water and squeeze excess water from the dipped cotton.
2. Gently press this soaked cotton on the palm, the trigger finger and the thumb of the accused. Store this water soaked cotton in a clean bottle, seal if for spectroscopic examination to prove that at the time of apprehension, gun powder was present on the hands of the accused. (It is important to note that separate such hand-washes should be taken from the left and the right hands of the accused.).
3. While sending the hand washes to the forensic laboratory, a control sample of the distilled water soaked cotton wool without the hand wash should also be sent to the forensic laboratory so that the Scientific Officer who examines the cotton wool can certify that the cotton wool used for removing the hand wash of the accused were from the same source and origin.

Detecting time of death

*E*stablishing the time of death of an individual animal can be a very important part of solving a wildlife crime. Time of death can be established by taking body temperature, ascertaining rigor mortis or by changes in the pupil of the eye.

A naso-pharyngeal thermometer if inserted into the nostril would give a temperature, which could be used to ascertain time of death. Many external factors can cause changes in the cooling of a carcass and this can differ between species. Rigor mortis or a post mortem state of rigidity may reverse after a certain time and may also vary with a number of external factors

A simple method for a crude estimation of time of death is by noting the physical changes in the eye. This could be in luminosity, shape, and loss of eye clarity, colour changes or constriction of the pupil.

Transparency and luminosity of the pupil decreases as time passes. The eye fluids turn cloudy and murky.

Eye shape changes from more rounded to more slit like as internal volumes of liquid are reduced and putrefaction sets in.

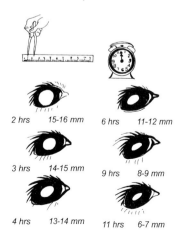

2 hrs	15-16 mm
3 hrs	14-15 mm
4 hrs	13-14 mm
6 hrs	11-12 mm
9 hrs	8-9 mm
11 hrs	6-7 mm

The diagram at the bottom of the left column illustrates pupil size for a dead deer. Pupil sizes of other groups of animals will differ.

1. First 30 minutes after death - eye lens and fluids fully transparent, light reflected from within the eye is a brilliant luminous green.Pupil size is dependent upon light intensity at the time of death. Shortly after death, the pupil is fully dilated as muscles relax.

2. From 30 minutes to 6 hours - lens and fluids remain transparent, luminosity and colour may decrease slightly, the fully dilated pupil is almost round (as rigor progresses the pupil gradually flattens). Fine, diagnostically insignificant wrinkles may be observed on eye surface.

3. From 6 to 10 hours - colour changes towards grey, luminosity fades, pupil width may decrease to about one-half original diameter.

4. From 12 to 18 hours - colour fades to dull grey, luminosity fades away, pupil may narrow to one-third or less of original diameter.

5. After 30 hours - colour and pupil diameter remain the same. Hazy blue colour will appear over brown iris after about 48 hours. Normally on the third to the sixth day after death, the eyeball has partially collapsed (depressions in the eye surface or sagging of eye away from eyelids). This condition is quite variable, hastened by dry wind and delayed by rain or high humidity.

Adapted from Gill and O'Meara (1965)

*M*ammalian teeth, and claws of both mammals and birds, are derivatives that often figure in the wildlife trade either individually (as in the instance of tiger teeth and claws worn as lockets) or in the form of artefacts, necklaces etc. Their identification is therefore important. Distinguishing them is also critical because teeth are very often found intact in old carcasses and can be used to identify the species.

➢ While species identification should be done by a qualified morphologist, these clues could help in the initial identification of the teeth upto a family or genus level.

Tiger canine

*Side of canine has one or more grooves which could be pitted
No rings on tip of enamel*

➢ The major difference in the dentition of carnivores and herbivores is the absence of canines in case of the latter. If complete sets of teeth are present, a distinct space between the incisors and the premolars (called the diastema) points to it being a herbivore.

➢ A carnivore canine can be differentiated into those belonging to bears (Ursidae) and cats (Felidae) by the help of the following diagram. The teeth of two families are the most common ones in the trade for use as ornaments or fetishes because of their symbolism and shape.

➢ Mammalian and avian claws can be very similar in external appearance. Mammalian claws (often called nails) and bird claws (often called talons) can be distinguished upto species level and their position on the foot and digit determined by an experienced examiner. The following tips are to distinguish it to the level of whether it belongs to a bird or a mammal

Bear canine

*Sides of canines have no grooves
Tips of enamel have fine brown rings*

Mammal claw   *Bird claw*

➤ Every claw consists of a bone (or digit) that is covered by a sheath of keratin (or unguis)

➤ Examine the ventral or underside. The mammalian claws are incompletely sheathed with keratin

➤ A separate sheath of keratin covers the underside completely.

➤ The two can also be told apart by the shape of the unguis and the bone in an X-Ray (see Diag)

Enforcement hints

1. All canines tend to crack longitudinally when dried

2. The teeth may be carved or faked (carved from bone or ivory) Look for carving marks. Check size and distinguishing features of real teeth.

Adapted from Beth Ann Sabo and Bonnie Yates, ID Notes, USFWS

Sexing a carcass using the pelvis

In certain mammals it is difficult to sex the carcass when external genitalia are absent in the carcass or when only bones remain because the carcass is found after a number of days after death.

The pelvis is a reliable way to sex such carcasses. The following three ways can help distinguish between male and female pelvises

1. The shape of the ischial arch is V in males and U in females. This is the easiest way to sex and can be made out in a carcass by feeling the pelvis through the skin and bone.

2. At the top of the ischial arc, males have a slight tubercle or bump (called the suspensory tubercle which the females lack)

3. The pubic arch is noticably thicker in males and can again be felt through the skin.

Male   *Female*   *Feeling thickness of Pubic Arch*

*I*t is often very important to differentiate wounds in carcasses while solving the most fundamental question in wildlife crime i.e. how has the animal died?

The six most common types of injuries are those caused by an arrow, a gun, by being run over by a vehicle, due to a fall, by traps or snares and by a predator.

Bullet wounds:

1. Contact wounds: These are wounds caused when a muzzle of a gun is held to the skin and then fired. Often the area is blackened with soot and the wound is very destructive.
2. Near contact wounds: These happen when the muzzle is held a short distance away and such wounds normally have a wider zone of soot over seared and blackened skin
3. Intermediate distance gunshot wounds: These have what is known as powder tattooing or the impact of unburned powder crystals on the skin in the form of reddish-brown dots or tattoos.
4. Distant gunshot wounds: This is caused by projectiles that are too far away to even cause tattooing.

Bullet wounds leave lead and or copper fragments in the wound which can be detected by a metal test, radiographs and at times metal detectors.

Note:

If bullet wound is administered after death the tattoo marks will be grey or yellow

Lead and copper tests can yield a false test in some cases.

Natural kills:

For distinguishing predator kills look for claw marks, feeding patterns and puncture wounds in the appropriate position (for example neck for cats, face and bowels for wild dogs etc.).

Check surrounding area for signs of predator including footprints and faecal remains.

Arrow wounds:

These are typical puncture wounds that are normally slightly triangular in shape. Normally, arrow wounds have extensive hemorrhaging around the margins of the wound (blood is clotted).

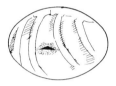

Unlike a bullet which shatters the flesh and bones around the point of entry, an arrow wound normally cuts through the flesh and bone. Less splinters and shattered pieces of surrounding tissue will be found.

Trauma wounds:

Trauma especially road accident victims are recognised by examining the exterior of the animal. Signs include large bruising, broken bones, tears in the body often with viscera protruding out and large areas of missing hair.

Remember that ribs that break can puncture the skin and make it look like a bullet wound.

Trapping wounds:

Look for trapping or snare wounds on leg, chest or neck which are the most common places for such wounds to occur.

The most indicative feature of a snare wound is the internal haemmorhaging which in most cases will be present. Even if the skin is not cut, evidence of bruising, haemmorhaging and deep depressions in the skin where the snare has taken hold will be present.

A post-mortem is invaluable for solving wildlife crimes. The following points may be kept in mind to achieve accurate reports.[6]

General pointers

1. Conduct the post-mortem in as sterile and clean a manner as possible. All personnel involved should wear surgical gloves. If possible masks should be worn.
2. Record points on paper or a tape-recorder as the operation is going on, and not later from memory.
3. Examine gut and stomach at the end to prevent spillage.
4. Examine all other organs for abnormalities.
5. Examine sub-cutaneous area for bruises, haemorrhages or burns.
6. Look in the abdominal and thoracic cavities for abnormal amount of fluid. Note its quantity, colour and consistency and collect sample in a test tube.
7. Look for parasites on surface of body, in body cavity and close to internal organs.
8. Examine respiratory system and lung for tumours, lesions, parasites etc. Cut a piece of the lung and let float in a basin of water for 15 minutes. The worms and parasites should sink to the bottom.
9. Check liver and gall bladder for abnormalities. Cut the liver in many places to look for pus or haemmorhage. Collect samples.
10. Examine heart and surrounding blood vessels. Note the consistency of blood in heart (clotted, semi-clotted, unclotted). Collect blood samples. Make one or two blood smears on glass slides.
11. Examine kidney and bladder. Collect sample. Collect urine sample for poison test.
12. Examine musculature for cysts and nematodes by cutting under the jaw, thigh etc. Take muscle samples if back-quarters disease is suspected.

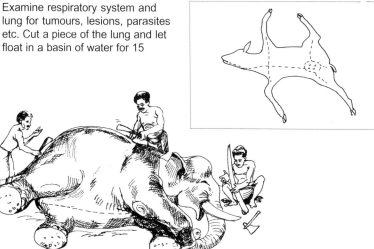

Elephant post-mortem being conducted; (inset) Dissection lines for ruminants

13. Examine reproductive organs. If female, check uterus for signs of past or currrent pregnancy. In case of abortion collect uterine fluid and part of endometrium.

14. Examine head cavity and brain. If rabies is suspected send entire head packed in ice to laboratory or at least 50% of the brain cut along the midline. Preserve in 50% buffered glycerine.

15. Examine all parts of digestive system from oesophagus and stomach to the intestines. In ruminants check rumen. Collect gut samples.

16. Collect tissue and blood samples separately for histological, pathological and toxicological tests. Take multiple samples.

17. Preserve samples in 10% formalin (for histopathology), in 50% buffered glycerine (for virology) and a few parts under refrigeration/ freezing (for microbiology). Borax is an alternative to refrigeration.

18. All samples must be labelled and

Packing samples for transportation

sealed properly.

19. Post-mortem reports must include photographs of different parts that have been examined, especially the parts which have provided the clinching evidence for the final result.

20. The final result must not be ambiguous such as 'natural cause' or 'weakness and illness'. A post-mortem report is a technical document and should be as precise as possible.

Some specific pointers for groups of animals

1. *Deer, antelope, wild cattle etc:*
   All ruminants must be dissected after being made to lie on the left side. This will avoid interference from the rumen.

2. *Horses, wild asses etc:*
   All equines must be dissected after being made to lie on the right side. This will avoid interference from the colon and caecum.

3. *Birds, small reptiles and mammals:*
   If small enough, these should be double packed in plastic bags, kept in a thermocole container and transported to a laboratory for post-mortem.

4. *Elephants and rhinos:*
   a) As these are very large animals, post-mortem should be done in the position that they were found in. Shift carcass if manpower is available.
   b) Tusks, horns etc are very valuable and must be measured and weighed. This should be recorded in the post-mortem report.

5. *Carnivores, bears, pigs:*
   All these animals can be placed on their back for the dissection.

Important: A post-mortem is to be done by a qualified veterinarian. The post-mortem report must be made available to concerned enforcement authorities.

*I*ndia has taken the bold step to include conservation and protection of environment in its national constitution, the highest law of the land. Article 48-A lays down that the "State shall endeavour to protect and improve the environment and to safeguard the forests and wildlife of the country." Article 51-A(g) of the constitution also imposes a duty on every citizen "to protect and improve the natural environment including forest and widlife". The Central statute on wildlife protection is the "Wildlife (Protection) Act, 1972 (WPA). Other significant statutes which are used to enforce environmental provisions include the Code of Criminal Procedure, the Indian Penal Code and the Customs Act. The basic ingredients to investigate and institute cases in respect of wildlife offence include *interalia,* the power conferred to authorised officers under the WPA, to enter, search, seize and arrest and file complaint.

1. Arresting power

The power of entry, search, arrest and detention are conferred under Section 50 of the WPA. Police officers not below the rank of sub-inspector have also been authorised under this Section.

2. Search/Seizure

Investigating officer should search the suspect, his premises and his vehicle. If prima-facie evidence of contraband is found, seize them and place them in safe custody. Then arrest the suspect. A receipt of such said articles be prepared and copy thereof be given to such person in the presence of two or more independent witnesses, and whose signatures should be obtained. The arresting officer should forthwith communicate to such persons the full particulars of the offence as well as the grounds for such an arrest.

3. Production

Immediately after the arrest, the concerned officer must produce the arrested person and the articles seized, within 24 hours, before the concerned Magistrate. Any person can also help law enforcement by acting as a law enforcement officer in case the crime is committed in front of the said individual. In this case private individuals can arrest, search and seize (u/s 43 CrPc) and file a report at the nearest police station provided the offence is cognizable and non-bailable.

4. Non bailable/bailable offence

Offences which are cognizable and punishable with imprisonment for three years or more are non-bailable and ones which are less than three years and non-cognizable are bailable.

5. Conditional bail

Prosecuting officer in the event of grant of bail to an accused must ensure that the Court in its order imposes a condition that the accused shall not commit an offence similar to the offence which he is accused of. Such a condition would be deterrent for the accused to further commit such offences and expedite the cancellation of bail already granted in case the accused commits another offence under the WPA.

6. Confession

Law does not permit recording a statement whether confessional or otherwise of an accused except in the presence of the designated Magistrate.

7. Recording statements as evidence

Any officer not below the rank of Asst. Director of Wildlife Preservation or the Wildlife Warden is authorised to record statements of witnesses as evidence to be used in Court provided:
a) Statement of the witness is recorded in the presence of the accused. b) Accused is given an opportunity to put questions, if any, to such witness. c) Witness to sign such statement. d) If the accused agrees then his signatures be also appended.

8. Complaint

A complaint is, any allegation made orally or in writing to a Magistrate, with a view to his taking action under Cr. P.C. against some person, whether known or unknown who has committed an offence. A complaint under WPA is made under Section 50 (4). Such complaint can be filed only by authorised officers under Section 55 of WPA. Members of the public can also file a wildlife court case by following the procedure under Section 55(c).

a) Format of Complaint

Law has not prescribed any specific format for drafting a complaint.

b) Contents of Complaint

Complaint must specify clearly detailed description of events, the source of the information; the enquiries made along with names of persons, places and details of the evidence collected, the instrument/weapon used.

c) Forensic Certificate

A document certifying the species of the animal/skin/animal article or plant seized is an essential ingredient of the documents that need to be filed in the Court.

d) Power to file a complaint

a) The Director of Wildlife Preservation or any other officer authorised on his behalf by the Central Government; or b) The Chief Wildlife Warden or any other officer authorised on his behalf by the state government; or c) Any person who has given notice of not less than 60 days, in the manner prescribed of the alleged offence. (Section 55 of WPA). The prescribed format has been appended under Wildlife Protection Rules, 1995.

e) Authorisation to file complaint

Complaint by an officer other than Director, Wildlife Preservation or Chief Wildlife Warden must be accompanied by a written order authorising such officer to file the complaint.

9. Role of Honorary Wildlife Wardens

Para 16 of Guidelines for Appointment of Honorary Wildlife Wardens stipulates that suitable HWWs can be authorised to file complaints in courts. HWWs should consult Chief Wildlife Warden of their state in this regard.

How to go to court

The following are steps in the prosecution of a wildlife criminal:

1) Power to enter, search any premises, vehicles, etc. and seize any wild animal article etc. (Section 50 of WPA).

2) Power to stop, detain or arrest any person without warrant (Section 50 WPA).

3) Recording of statement of the witnesses to the offence by Assistant Director of Wildlife Preservation or by Wildlife Warden (Section 50(d) of WPA).

4) To produce the arrested person and articles seized before the concerned Magistrate ((Section 50(g) of WPA).

5) Bail/Conditional grant of bail (Section 437(3)(b) CrPc).

6) Authorisation to file complaint (Section 55 of WPA).

7) Filing of complaint (Section 55 WPA read with Section 190 (CrPc).

8) Examination of the authorised person presenting the complaint to be dispensed with (Section 200 (CrPc).

9) Issuance of warrants/summons by Magistrate to the accused along with the copy of complaint (Section 204 CrPc).

10) Recording of Pre-charge evidence (Section 244 CrPc).

11) Framing of charge (Section 246 of CrPc).

12) Accused to state whether pleads guilty or not guilty of such charge (Section 246(2) of CrPc).

13) Accused pleads not guilty, then witnesses whose statement had been recorded earlier to be summoned for cross examination by the accused (Section 246(4) CrPc).

14) Accused to enter upon his defence and produce his evidence (Section 247 CrPc).

15) Examination of the accused by court. Accused has right to refuse to answer such questions (Section 313 CrPc).

16) Submission of arguments (Section 314 CrPc).

17) Judgement: acquittal or conviction of the accused (Section 248 CrPc).

18) Submission of arguments or quantum of sentence, in event of conviction (Section 248 CrPc).

19) Pronouncement of sentence/fine by court (Section 248 CrPc) in presence of accused. Accused to be sent to jail to undergo sentence.

20) Appeal.

*A*n important element of a seizure is the disposal of the seized contraband. In most cases, this can be done only after the final court proceedings are completed. In other cases, especially when it is a live animal, different procedures must be followed.

Options for disposal

a) **Dead Specimens, Parts and Derivatives:**
- Donation to museums and Forensic labs. for scientific research.
- Use for training and educational purposes.
- Storage.
- Destruction. This is the recommended option. Display of wildlife articles can encourage demand.

b) **Live Specimens:**
- Return to country of origin.
- Transfer to a rescue center/ zoo.
- Return to the wild.

- Euthanasia.
- If a live animal or plant is involved, remember that the survival and the security of the animal or plant should be paramount.
- Seizures of wildlife should be brought to the attention of wildlife officers as soon as possible. Decisions of disposal should be made in agreement with the management authority.
- A list of addresses to contact for disposal of specimens is given on page 105-107

✚ Warning

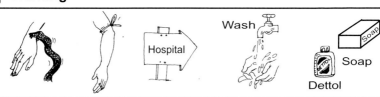

Wildlife crime and militant organisations

- Militant and extremist groups often poach and trade in wildlife as a means of accumulating cash for arms.
- This is especially difficult to deal with as militants are usually better armed than poachers and are often better organised.
- In India, a number of terrorist groups have been implicated in wildlife trading and poaching. Some groups actively combated poaching at one time, killing poachers as anti-social elements. This, however, is rare.
- Wildlife enforcement officers must take the help of appropriate law and order agencies in such cases.

An investigator must first determine whether the product being examined is organic or not, i.e. whether it is of animal or plant origin as compared to plastic, synthetic materials, etc.

1. Wildlife trade items come in many different forms. Look at the item carefully in artificial light and sunlight. Use a magnifying glass if necessary. Note texture, shine, patterns, etc.

2. If possible cut or break off a small part of the object

3. Burn the part. Organic matter smells of burnt hair. Synthetic material smells like burnt plastic.

Wildlife crime and narcotics

➢ Wildlife smugglers and drug barons often operate hand in hand. In some cases, they are one and the same.

➢ In Kerala, the *ganja* (hashish) cultivators and smugglers also control ivory poaching. In North-East India, the biggest live-animal trader is also a gun-runner and a drug smuggler.

➢ At some international borders, such as the Indo-Myanmar border, open bartering of wildlife for narcotics, pharmaceutical prescriptions, drugs, arms and prostitutes takes place.

➢ Snakes are used for 'couriering' drugs internationally. In June 1993, a shipment of 103 boa snakes from Colombia to USA was detected by X-ray to have been stuffed with cocaine-filled condoms. Always X-ray suspicious wildlife goods.

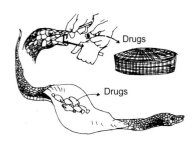

Bears

➤ The Himalayan black bear
(*Selenarctos thibetanus)* and the
sloth bear (*Melursus ursinus)* are
commonly killed for their gall
bladders.[3]

➤ Himalayan black bear numbers are
unknown but the sloth bear
population is between 5000-7000
and believed to be declining.[7]

➤ The bears are poached by laying
leg-hold traps, by shooting or by
capturing as cubs (see section on
Live Mammals, page 68).

➤ Rotting fruits, especially pumpkin
and jackfruit, are used as bait.

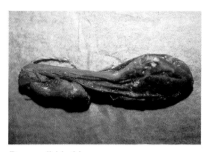

Bear gall bladder

Bear bile

➤ There is trade in whole gall bladders
(*pith* in Hindi) and crystallised bear
bile (sometimes sulphur-yellow
when frozen).[8]

➤ Bear bile is used in Oriental medicines in the Far-east, especially
Korea, China, Japan and Taiwan[9]
for digestive disorders.

➤ It generally follows the trade centres
and routes of musk.

➤ In India it is used in Tibetan and
Ayurvedic medicines.

➤ Bear paws, meat and fat are also in
the trade.[9]

*Bear gall bladders in trade — flattened
(L), whole (R) and bile grains*

Enforcement tips

➤ Bear gall bladders and bear bile can
be confused with those of pigs,
sheep and cows. They cannot be
identified by sight, smell or taste.
See Annexure-III for identification
techniques.

➤ Often smuggled as frozen food that
sometimes resembles processed
cheese. These consignments
should be checked.[8]

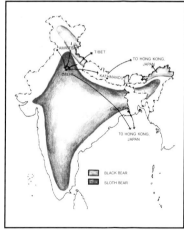

*Distribution of bears and trade routes of
bear bile*

Musk deer

> The musk deer is a high altitude deer found in pockets in India, Nepal and Bhutan in the Himalayas (extralimitally also in the Russian Federation, China and North Korea).

> It has a population of less than 50,000 in the Himalayas (perhaps maybe as low as 30,000). The numbers are declining rapidly due to poaching and trade.

> Musk comes from a gland in the abdominal region of the male musk deer. Musk from the Himalayas is obtained by killing the deer as there are no farms producing commercial musk in this region.[3]

> Three farms do exist in the western Himalayas but due to various limitations, they do not produce musk commercially.

> Poaching is done by traps (foot snares) and by shooting. The first method is entirely indiscriminate, killing adult males, females and immatures.

> The musk deer is listed as endangered by IUCN, in Schedule-I of WPA and Appendix-I of CITES.

Musk

> Musk or *kasturi* is a very expensive natural perfume fixative. It is also used in Asian medicine.

> Domestically it is used in the Ayurveda, Unani and Tibetan schools of medicine for a large number of remedies. Outside India it is used extensively in the Chinese medicine system.

> Musk is traded as whole pods, musk grain and in liquid form. The pods are traded as 'catties'. One catty contains

Musk deer in the Himalayas

630 gms of musk or the pods from about 24 male musk deer.[10]

Enforcement tips

> Musk deer are poached throughout the Himalayas. Winter is the peak season. Substantial poaching is done by local villagers, who are supported by a well-knit trade collection system.

> Foot snares and leg-hold traps placed throughout the Himalayan forests need to be detected and removed.

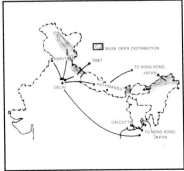

Distribution of musk deer and trade routes of musk

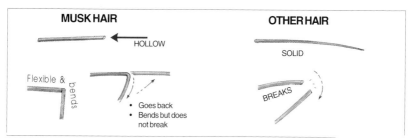

MUSK HAIR	OTHER HAIR

- HOLLOW
- SOLID
- Flexible & bends
- Goes back
- Bends but does not break
- BREAKS

Identification of hair of musk deer from other mammalian hairs

- ➤ In case of a seizure of a pod, check if it is brownish in colour, oval to circular in shape and slightly flattened. Fake pods have either wrong shape or colour (see Fakes). For hair, see illustration.
- ➤ Check if real pod is filled with fake musk by looking for cut marks at the base or by checking for syringe marks used to extract genuine musk.[3]
- ➤ In case of musk grain or liquid, use a laboratory test. Traders use a 'home-test' by dipping or rubbing a piece of string in asafoetida (*hing*, a spice) and then onto musk. Only genuine musk will mask the smell of asafoetida.[11]

- ➤ In the Far East, genuine musk is said to remain as granules in water and become molten liquid on live charcoal. Fakes would melt in water and char on charcoal.[12]
- ➤ The musk trade is controlled by one family based in Hong Kong, Nepal and India. Land routes to Nepal from India and air traffic to Hong Kong from India, Nepal and Bhutan are most vulnerable.
- ➤ Apart from musk deer, musk is also obtained from civet cats. This comes mostly from the small Indian civet (*Viverricula indica*) and the large Indian civet (*Viverra zibetha*).

Fake musk pods for sale in Japan

Asian elephant - Elephas maximus

Poached elephant in Mudumalai sanctuary

Asian elephant

➤ There are approximately 40,000 Asian elephants in 13 range countries. More than half of these (i.e. 25,000-27,000) are found in India.[13] In comparison there are 250,000 elephants in Africa.

➤ Among Asian elephants, only the males have tusks. Females have short tushes, not valued by the trade. There are also tuskless males or *makhnas*.

➤ In India, poaching has been a major, escalating concern for the last two decades. More than 100 tuskers were recorded as poached in 1997.[14] The male-female ratio in some parts of southern India is 1:100 (normal ratio is 1:3 or 1:4).[13]

➤ The Asian elephant is listed as endangered by the IUCN, in Schedule-I of WPA and Appendix-I of CITES.

Ivory

➤ Ivory is obtained primarily from the tusks of the two living elephant species and the extinct mammoth (from fossils), although dentine from the tusk or teeth of hippopotamus, walrus, and narwahl is also called ivory. Whale, fish and camel bone are often used in the trade as substitues.

➤ The tusk is a functional part of an elephant (used in feeding, defence, etc) and should not be removed from a wild elephant. Also, as it is a tooth and has a large living part (with blood vessels and nerves), the tusk should not be cut except at the tip, from a living elephant.

➤ The average weight of an Asian elephant tusk is around 10 kg although this is decreasing as poachers have killed off many of the larger and older tuskers.[14]

➤ Traders differentiate soft and hard ivory as originating from grassland and forest elephants respectively. Some traders believe that Indian (or Asian) ivory is easier to carve on. Asian ivory fetches a higher price than African ivory.[14]

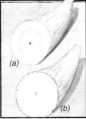

Differences between hard(a) & soft(b) ivory

Ivory

Enforcement tips

➤ Ivory can be differentiated from bone by putting a flame to. Ivory blackens but does not char like bone (unless a very high temperature is used). (see illustration).

➤ Ivory also has distinctive hatch markings which can be seen if you look closely at an unpolished part of the surface.[15]

➤ For positive identification and also separation between species, laboratory tests (using Schreger lines) are required. (see Annexure-VI).[15]

➤ Traders feel that hard ivory has a 'skin' and a core and also that it develops less cracks than soft ivory. This is unscientific but can give clues to the origin of the tusks.

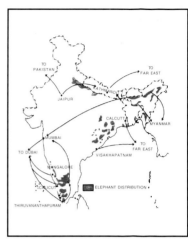

Distribution of elephants and trade routes of ivory

Mammoth, African and Asian elephant

Ivory and bone statues

Bone chars on putting a flame to it. Ivory does not

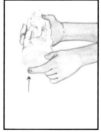

Look at underside (unpolished)

Bone has lines. Ivory has hatch marks

Rhino horn

Greater one-horned rhino

➤ The greater one-horned rhinoceros (*Rhinoceros unicornis*) is one of five species of rhinos in the world, three of which are found in Asia and two in Africa.

➤ There are about 2,000 one-horned rhinos left in the wild of which approximately 1,500 are in India and 500 in Nepal. In India, more than 1,000 rhinos are in Kaziranga National Park in Assam and the remaining are spread over in seven sites in Assam, West Bengal and Uttar Pradesh.[16]

➤ Due to the rhino horn trade, all five species of rhino in the world are endangered.

➤ The rhino is listed as endangered species by the IUCN and is protected under Schedule-I of WPA and Appendix-I of CITES.

➤ Rhinos are poached mostly by shooting, although pit poaching and poisoning are used as well. There is also an ingenious method of electro-cution whereby a live wire connected to a high tension line is left dangling on a known rhino *dandi* (path). The rhino is electrocuted on contact.

Rhino horn

➤ The Asian rhino is poached only for its horn which is smuggled to the Far East for use in Oriental medicine (to reduce fever, for treating paralysis and high blood pressure, and sometimes in the mistaken belief that it is an aphrodisiac).

➤ Rhino horn is usually smuggled out of India in one piece although sometimes chips and powder might be exported for use in Tibetan medicine.[16]

➤ It is considered more valuable as a medicine and it fetches five times the price of African rhino horn.

➤ The mean weight of an Indian rhino horn is 700-800 gms.[17]

Greater one-horned rhinoceros in Kaziranga

Enforcement tips

➤ Convincing fake rhino horns are made from cattle and buffalo horn, bamboo root, resin and occasionally carved from bone and wood. Rare cases of stone and ivory being used have also been documented.[16]

➤ Rhino horn is condensed hair. If a piece is burned it will smell of burning hair.

➤ The base of a rhino horn has numerous pores (canaliculi). This can be faked effectively only in bamboo root which will not however smell like burning hair.

➤ There are two distinct layers to some fake horns (e.g. those made of wood and resin). The outer layer will chip or peel.

➤ African rhino horns are by and large much bigger and more curved than Asian horns. This is, however, not a foolproof test. There is also a difference in the base of the white and black rhino horns, the former being more rectangular in the outline and the latter more circular.[18]

➤ Regularly verify existing rhino-horn stocks. There is a possibility that traders might gain access to rhino-horn stocks. If possible destroy the

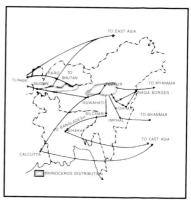

Distribution of rhinoceros and trade routes of rhino horns

horns after verification.

➤ Check rhino *dandis* regularly for pits and electrical line traps.

➤ Be alert specially during monsoon when floods may drive rhinos to high-lying, less protected areas.

➤ Dimapur town of Nagaland is a major illegal rhino-horn trade centre, as is Siliguri in West Bengal. These are important trade routes to Myanmar, Bhutan and Nepal respectively.

Rhino horn for sale in South Korea

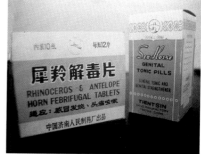

Rhino-horn tablets

Tiger and leopard

➤ Two of the most endangered animals in India are the tiger and the leopard.

➤ While there are between 3,000-4,000 tigers in India, the number of leopards is unknown.

➤ Loss of habitat used to be the single largest threat to the future of wild tigers in India. It is now clear that the trade in tiger bones is contributing to pushing the tiger to near extinction.[19]

➤ The leopard is more widely distributed than the tiger and is found near villages and towns.

➤ For one tiger skin, six to seven leopard skins are seized showing that the leopard is hunted more than the tiger.

➤ Leopard populations vary widely. At some places there are too many, at others very few.

➤ The main areas of tiger poaching are in the states of Madhya Pradesh, Uttar Pradesh, West Bengal, Bihar, Maharashtra, Andhra Pradesh and Karnataka.[19]

➤ Poachers use poison, steel traps and firearms to kill a tiger or leopard.

Tiger and leopard parts

➤ Earlier, tigers and leopards were killed for their skins.

➤ Investigations carried out in 1992-94, during which a total of 36 tiger skins and 667 kg of tiger bones were seized in North India, revealed the new demand for tiger and leopard bones.[19]

➤ These parts are used to manufacture traditional Chinese medicine which is sold clandestinely in the Far East and many Western countries.

Tiger skull and bones

➤ Tiger bones are used as a general tonic in tiger-bone wine, to cure rheumatism, and in tiger-bone plasters.

➤ Tiger bone is also used for removing all kinds of evil influences and calming fright, for curing bad ulcers, for muscle cramps, abdomi- nal pain, typhoid fever, malaria, and hydrophobia. It is said to strengthen the bones, cure chronic dysentery and prolapse of the anus. The powdered bone is applied to burns.

➤ The Majestic bone of a tiger also called floating bone, is one inch long, and grows on each side of the chest by the ribs. This is worn by officials for poise and confidence.

➤ Besides tiger bone, the following parts of the tiger are also used in Chinese medicine: tiger flesh, fat, stomach, testes, bile, eyeball, nose, teeth,

Leopard skin and bones

stomach (*Tu*), testes (*Shen*), bile (*Tan*), eyeball (*Ching*), nose (*Pi*), teeth (*Ya*), claws (*Chao*), skin (*P'i*), whiskers (*Hsu*), faeces (*Shih*), bones in faeces (*Shih Chung Ku*), blood (*Hsush*) and penis.[20]

➢ In India generally skin, bones, claws and teeth are taken from a poached tiger.

➢ Although tiger parts are the most valuable, other cat parts can be used as substitutes in traditional medicine. This includes parts of the leopard, snow leopard and golden cat.

➢ A favoured route of smuggling from India is overland to Tibet or via Nepal where the bones are usually bartered for shahtoosh or down hair of the Tibetan antelope or chiru. (see page 62).[21]

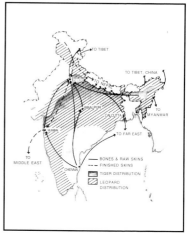

Distribution of tiger & leopard and trade routes of their parts

Enforcement tips

➢ Ownership certificates for old tiger and leopard skins, issued by the forest department, should be checked regularly by the authorities. These are often used illegally to safely store fresh skins.[19]

➢ After appropriate permission from the courts, the seized wildlife products should be collected and destroyed. There is evidence that because of their high value and demand seized goods are tampered with and re-enter the market (tiger and leopard bones in particular cannot be easily identified).

➢ A large number of fake skins,claws and teeth are in the market. The skins are normally dog or cow hides and may be distinguished by simple examination. Fake claws and teeth are usually fashioned out of buffalo horn or dog canines. (see page 94)

➢ The legal trade in cattle bones for fertilisers, glue and gelatin needs to be carefully monitored.[19]

➢ Tiger skins are bought by collectors in India or are smuggled to Europe, USA and the Middle-East.

Tiger-bone wine being sold in Japan

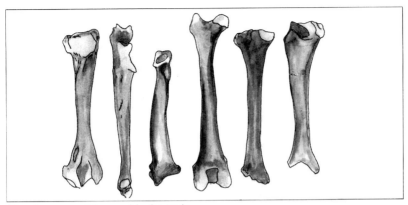

Tiger bones most favoured in the trade

- Identification of the four limb bones, namely, the humerus, radius, ulna and femur, is very important to distinguish them from other animal bones. (see illustration).
- For identification of claws the best way is to take an X-ray (see illustration). If it is a genuine claw, the bony part will go into the skin, forming a keel. Also look for small chisel marks which are pointers that a claw has been made from horn or other materials.
- To identify fake skins, look at the pattern carefully to see if it matches that of a real tiger. Wipe the black stripes with cotton wool soaked in perming lotion to see if they smudge. Pluck a black hair (longest available) and see if it is black upto its roots. Check for size and whether distinguishing parts such as the tail, head etc. are intact.

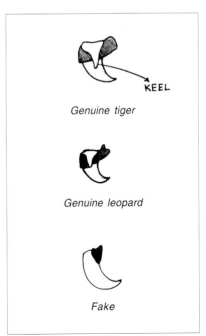

Genuine tiger

Genuine leopard

Fake

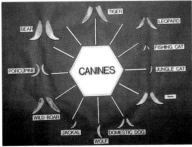

Tiger canines with teeth of other animals

Tiger claw identification

Fur

Fur-yielding species

➤ The fur trade in India deals with 20 wild caught species of which 18 are endangered or vulnerable.[1]

➤ The global demand for fur coats, rugs and fashion accessories made from mammalian fur threatens species belonging to the wild cat, dog, otter and weasel families.

➤ Among the big cats, the tiger, snow leopard, leopard, and clouded leopard are hunted for their fur.

➤ Lesser cats like desert cat, fishing cat, jungle cat and leopard cat enter the trade in the thousands.[1]

➤ Species such as jackal, fox and wolf and other species such as otters, weasels and civets form the rest of the trade.

Fur trade

➤ The trade in fur mainly operates out of North and North-East India with Jammu and Kashmir being an important processing centre.

➤ Limited domestic trade is allowed in species like mink and Angora rabbits which are captive-bred, but all trade in wild fur is illegal.

➤ The market for furs is limited to big cities and hill stations within India. The goods are also smuggled to other destinations in Asia (including Nepal and East European countries).

Enforcement tips

➤ The Jammu and Kashmir Wildlife (Protection) Act, 1978 allows trade in the skins of certain species which are banned in the rest of India. Skins from other parts of India are taken there, stitched into coats and

A live fishing cat. 20-40 skins make one coat

smuggled out again.[22]

➤ Fur can be smuggled as untanned skin or as a finished garment. The former might be smuggled with legal leather, suede and cattle skin. The latter is carried in hand baggage or smuggled with clothing, blankets etc.

➤ A number of fakes, especially of tiger and leopard skins, are in the market (see Fakes, page 94). Fur coats made of domestic cat and legal mink are also on sale.

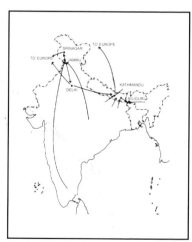

Trade routes of furs

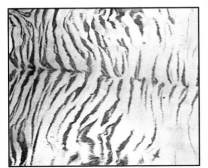

Tiger skin

Leopard skin

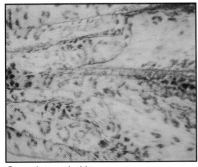

Snow leopard skin

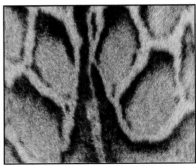

Clouded leopard skin

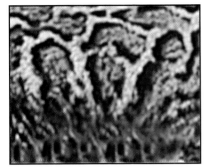

Marble cat skin

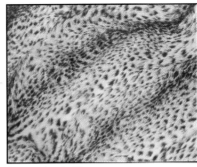

Leopard cat skin

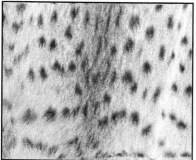

Desert cat skin

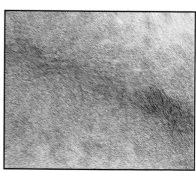

Jungle cat skin

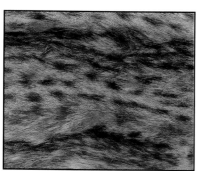

Fishing cat skin

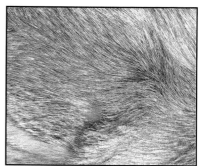

Red fox skin

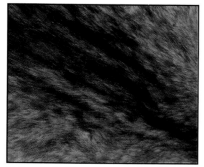

Palm civet skin

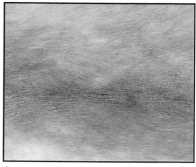

Stone marten skin

▲ *Tibetan antelope or chiru in Tibet*

◀ *A model wearing shahtoosh and pashmina shawls*

The Tibetan antelope or *chiru*

> The Tibetan antelope or *chiru* (*Pantholops hodgsoni*) is endemic to the Tibetan Plateau. It is largely found in the high pastures of the Chang Tang. During the summer months a small population migrates to north-eastern Ladakh in India.[21]
> Population estimates in 1995 were a maximum of 75,000 animals.[21]
> The *chiru* is hunted for its down wool (shahtoosh), meat (for local consumption) and horns (for Tibetan medicine).
> Poaching is threatening *chiru* populations throughout its range.

Shahtoosh shawls

> *Shahtoosh* means 'king of wool'. It is the finest natural fibre in the world.
> Shahtoosh or 'ring' shawls are heirlooms in northern India. They are woven exclusively in the state of Jammu and Kashmir.
> Shahtoosh is the down wool of the *chiru*. The animals are killed for the collection of wool. They have not been raised in captivity.[21] In contrast,

pashmina (the most common woollen shawl of India) comes from the wool of the domestic goat.
> The cost of shahtoosh wool is upto thirty times that of pashmina wool.[21]
> The main buyers today are not traditional Indians but fashion crazed people in Europe, North America, the Far East, Middle East and even Australia and South Africa.
> New techniques to develop a finer pashmina shawl are being developed as an alternative to shahtoosh.

Enforcement tips

> Shahtoosh is exceptionally soft, with a feather-light quality that is absent in other wool including pashmina. On-site identification by touch becomes more difficult when it is compared to cashmere or blended fine wool. The human skin can sense the difference upto one micron.[21]
> Look at a shahtoosh guard hair (the longest hair, also known as kemp hair), under a magnifying glass. It has inherent crinkles in it. Pashmina is much straighter (see Fakes, page

94).

Hints about the shawl being shahtoosh are:

a) The price (anything over Rs20,000 should be examined).

b) The colour (normally off-white to beige, although dyed shahtoosh shawls are now being seen).

c) The embroidery (shawls are usually plain or with minimum embroidery).

d) The signature (usually the craftsman stitches his initials in a corner of the shawl).

Passing through a ring is not exclusively a shahtoosh trait; even fine pashmina can do this.

Positive identification is possible by examining a hair under a microscope (see illustration).

Shahtoosh guard hair is distinctive under a microscope. The medulla of the hair comprises round cells in a lattice formation. Also, the diameter of the fibre is between 6-10 micron while pashmina is normally between 13-15 micron. Shawls are often woven in a pattern of small diamonds known as 'chashme bulbul' ('eye of the bulbul').

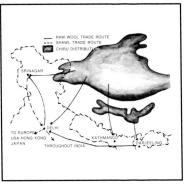

Distribution of chiru and trade routes of shahtoosh wool and shawls

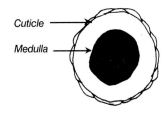

Sample hair under a microscope

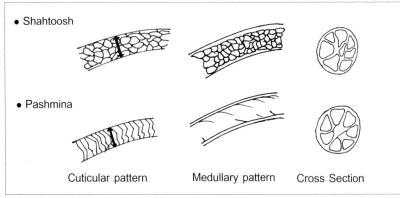

- Shahtoosh
- Pashmina

Cuticular pattern   Medullary pattern   Cross Section

Shahtoosh and pashmina hair under a microscope[23]

Reptile skins

Reptiles in skin trade

➤ The ratsnake, often referred to as whipsnake, is the most common snake in the trade. More than half the skins in the Indian trade are from this non-poisonous species.

➤ The cobra, the saw-scaled viper, Russell's viper, keelbacks, etc., are also in the trade. Python skin is rarer but much sought after.

➤ The decline of the ratsnake, which is a natural pest control, is causing serious grain storage problems and consequent loss to the national exchequer.

➤ Two species of crocodile and three species of monitor lizards are also greatly prized by the trade.

➤ All crocodiles, pythons and the yellow monitor lizard are given maximum protection by WPA and CITES. Other monitor lizards and snakes are protected in various schedules of the WPA.

Skin trade

➤ When the trade was legal, annual Indian exports of reptile skins used to be worth US $ 60 million. In 1977, India exported 4 million snake skins. Today all trade is banned.[1]

➤ The world trade in lizard skins was 1 million and in crocodile skins 2 million

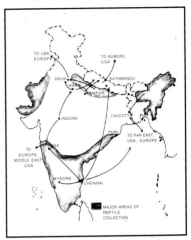

Reptile skin trade routes

annually.[1]

➤ Reptile skins are used in the fashion accessory trade of handbags, wallets, boots, belts etc.

➤ Skins are either tanned in places such as Chennai, Agra and Pune or sold raw and untanned.

➤ Prices for reptile skin are fixed depending on the species and the width of the skin. Length is rarely the consideration.

Enforcement tips

➤ Skins may be smuggled out with consignments of leather, garments or hides. Check these carefully.

➤ To identify a genuine skin, rub a coin or key against the scales of the skin. In snakes and lizards the scales will lift up, while in embossed plastic or other artificial material they will not.

➤ Crocodile scales do not lift like snake skins. Burn a small portion. It will smell of burning hair.

Reptile skins stacked for sale, New Delhi

Reptile skins

Species	Neck	Body	Ventral	Caudal	Average
Vipera russelli	27-33	21-23	153-180	41-64	
Xenochrophis piscator	19	19	140-154	63-76	
Ptyas mucosus	17-19	16-17	190-213	100-146	
Naja naja naja	25-35	21-25	176-200	48-75	
Naja naja kaouthia	25-31	19-21	164-196	43-58	
Naja naja oxiana	23-27	21-23	186-213	62-75	
Ophiophagus hannah	17-19	15	240-254	84-104	
Python molurus	60-75	60-75	245-270	58-73	
Varanus bengalensis					90-110
Varanus flavescens					65-75
Varanus salvator					80-95

Scale count for common Indian reptiles in trade

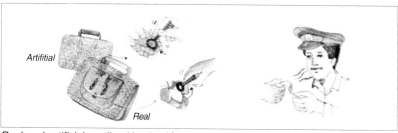

Artifitial

Real

Real and artificial reptile skin check[3]

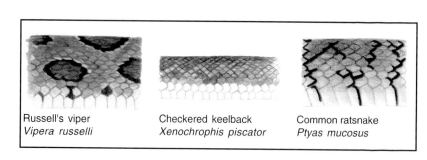

Russell's viper
Vipera russelli

Checkered keelback
Xenochrophis piscator

Common ratsnake
Ptyas mucosus

Common cobra
Naja naja

Indian python
Python molurus

Banded krait
Bungarus caeruleus

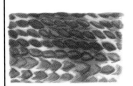

King cobra
Ophiophagus hannah

Water monitor lizard
Varanus salvator

Common monitor lizard
Varanus bengalensis

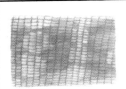

Yellow monitor lizard
Varanus flavescens

Marsh crocodile
Crocodylus palustris

Salt water crocodile
Crocodylus porosus

Live reptiles

Reptile species
- Species of snakes and tortoises are commonly traded as pets both in domestic and international markets.
- The star tortoise (*Geochelone elegans*), roofed turtle (*Kachuga tecta*), pond turtle (*Melanochelys trijuga*), python (*Python molurus*). cobra (*Naja naja*), king cobra (*Ophiophagus hannah*) and spiny-tailed lizard (*Uromastyx hardwickii*) are the most commonly traded live species.[3]
- All species are protected under Indian law and are endangered or vulnerable.

Live trade
- The snakes are used by snake charmers for road-side shows and by research institutions requiring snake venom.
- Turtles are kept as pets and used for medicine and food.
- The spiny-tailed lizard is sold for use in traditional medicine as an aphrodisiac. These lizards are starved for days on end, their backs broken to prevent escape, and are finally boiled alive in oil.
- The star tortoise and snakes such as

Snake charmer with cobras

the python and the king cobra are in great demand in the pet trade internationally and are smuggled out.[3]

Enforcement tips
- Live snakes and tortoises may be carried by the person concealed in his or her clothing, etc. They may be hidden in hand baggages or checked in, as these animals can survive low temperature and live without food and water for long periods.
- Be extremely careful while handling live reptiles. Many snakes are poisonous and most of the snakes, turtles and lizards can inflict serious wounds even if they are not poisonous (see page 95).

Spiny tailed lizards being sold in New Delhi

Species in trade

➢ Most common in the live mammal trade are primates or monkeys. In the domestic trade, rhesus (*Macaca mulatta*) and bonnet macaques (*Macaca radiata*) are often used as performing monkeys on the streets. The common langur (*Presbytis entellus*) is also sometimes held in captivity.

➢ The demand for wild-caught rhesus from India was an important reason for the ban on monkey export in the 1970s. This species was used exclusively for medical research in Europe and the Americas. Even today nearly 80%-90% of the primates used in research come from the wild.[1]

➢ The live mammals that are smuggled into markets in South-East Asia include primates such as the hoolock gibbon (*Hylobates hoolock*), the slow and slender loris (*Nycticebus coucang* and *Loris tardigradus*), the pig-tailed macaque (*Macaca nemestrina*), etc.

➢ Trapping of live bear cubs for use as performing bears, and of almost any live mammal by zoos, are well known. Smuggling of bears into Pakistan for staging bear fights is also on record.

Monkey charmer and performing rhesus

Live mammal trade

➢ The trade is largely based in Mir Shikar Toli in Patna, Bihar. Traders and trappers here exert tremendous influence over their brethren nationwide.

➢ The main demand for this trade is from zoos, circuses, illegal animal holdings, and for supply to the food and medicine markets of South-East Asia. There is also a large demand for exotic pets.

➢ In the North-East, the live animal trade is based in Assam and Meghalaya. Land routes to Myanmar are often used. In many cases, the animals are bartered for other illegal contraband including narcotics, arms etc.

➢ Travelling zoos are now banned in India and any such collection of animals is illegal.

➢ Most international airlines no longer carry live mammals or birds.

➢ The trade focuses on young and juvenile animals. In most cases the mother is shot before the

Techniques of smuggling live mammals

young ones are taken away. In others, leg-hold traps and snares are used to capture the animal.

Enforcement tips

➢ Check vulnerable areas for leg traps, nooses and snares. These must be found and destroyed at regular intervals by foot patrols. (see page 28).

➢ Land borders are crucial for smuggling live mammals between countries. The animals are rarely taken by air.

➢ Live mammals may be smuggled with domestic species, normally cattle or sheep being taken in and out of remote villages in trucks or lorries. The smell and noise of the domestic animals can confuse law enforcement officers.

➢ Small mammals such as lorises and pangolins may be hidden in consignments of poultry. The birds cause the animal to curl into a ball and be silent.

➢ In many cases, a crude anaesthetic is administered to the animal while transporting. This can be as basic as crushed onion tied over the nostril, or even narcotic preparations.

➢ Always be careful. Even small mammals can bite and draw blood. Handle only if trained. Do not over stress the animal in case of confiscation.

➢ Always consult wildlife scientist and local conservationists for re-introduction of small mammals in the appropriate area. Don't simply release animals in the area where they were confiscated. They may not belong there.

➢ There is much cruelty involved in the capture, training, transportation and final display of live animals. In case of confiscation, the Prevention of

Slow loris: a favourite pet species

Cruelty to Animals Act, 1960 may also be used, alone or in conjunction with other legislations.

➢ Focus checks on cargo of airlines that fly to destinations in South-East Asia, the Middle East and Europe and which do not have a policy of banning transport of live animals.

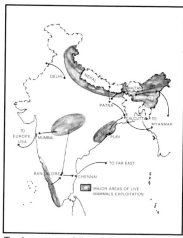

Trade routes of live mammals

Live birds

Species in trade

- A fifth of the world's bird species are in the international trade, of which 6% belongs to endangered species.[1]
- There are approximately 500 Indian bird species in the trade.
- Species caught for food include wild ducks, geese, assorted waterfowl, junglefowl, partridges, quails, pheasants, doves, and pigeons.
- Species caught for keeping as personal pets include parakeets, hill myna, munias etc. Parakeets may be the rose-ringed (*Psittacula krameri*), the alexandrine (*Psittacula eupatria*), the blossom-headed (*Psittacula cyanocephala*) and the red-breasted (*Psittacula alexandri*). Common munias are the red (*Estrilda amandava*), the spotted (*Lonchura punctulata*), the white-throated (*Lonchura malabarica*) and the white-rumped (*Lonchura striata*).[24]
- For zoos, larger and more colourful birds such as hornbills, flamingoes, storks, pheasants, cranes, ducks etc., are caught.
- Species such as owls, hornbills etc are used in witchcraft and medicine.
- Many raptors including hawks and falcons such as the peregrine (*Falco p. peregrinus*), shaheen (*Falco p. shaheen*) and the red-headed merlin (*Falco chiquera*) are in the trade for falconry. In some areas bird fights are a popular sport and involves capture of partridges, quails etc.
- For ornamental purposes colourful birds and song birds such as the bulbul, the shama and the munia are used.
- Some religions such as

Shaheen falcon on falconer's wrist

Jainism and Buddhism encourage the release of birds on certain days. This involves the capture of doves, pigeons, mynas, bulbuls, rollers etc. Instead of piety this leads to bird mortality.[24]

Bird trade

- Birds are traded for one of the following reasons: as food, as pets, for zoos, for ornamental purposes, for use in medicine, for sport, and for religious reasons.

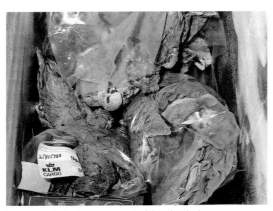

Live parrots being transported in plastic bags

Live birds

➤ Between 1970-1976, 13 million birds were exported from India.[1]
➤ Of these 80% comprised either parakeets or munias.
➤ The export of live birds from India was banned in 1990.
➤ The domestic trade of Indian species was banned in 1991. This includes parakeets, munias, mynas etc.
➤ Only some exotic species (species not from India such as budgerigar, macaws, cockatoo etc) can be sold and that, too, only with a licence.
➤ Major exporting countries in the global trade are India, China, Pakistan, Thailand, Bangladesh, Indonesia, Nepal, Philippines, Senegal, Paraguay and Bolivia.
➤ Major importing countries in the global trade are USA, Japan, Germany, Belgium, France, Netherlands and UK.
➤ There is significant mortality in the bird trade including during trapping, transport, the initial stage of purchase and quarantine.

Enforcement tips

➤ Live birds are smuggled out largely by concealment, either through land borders or by air, in false bottom suitcases, hollow tubes, etc.

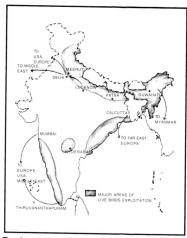

Trade routes of live birds

➤ When a small number is being smuggled, the value of individual birds will be very high.
➤ Live birds can be detected by trained sniffer dogs if these are available to the agency.
➤ Chicks often go with domestic poultry chicks, e.g. peacock chicks with cut crests accompany chicks of domestic hens.
➤ Eggs containing potential live birds may often be strapped to the body of a courier. In cases of rare parrots these eggs may be extremely valuable.

Smuggling techniques for live birds

Turtles

Olive ridley turtle in southern India

Turtles

➤ India has 26 species of freshwater turtles and tortoises and 5 species of marine turtles. Of these 31 species, 25 are exploited to varying degrees.[25]

➤ Turtles are largely aquatic reptiles while tortoises are terrestrial.

➤ Turtles are poached for food (meat, eggs and fat), keeping as pets, traditional medicines and for commerically used derivatives such as tortoiseshell, stuffed carapaces, leather etc.

➤ All the marine turtles are endangered while more than a dozen freshwater turtles are also endangered.

➤ The olive ridley, hawksbill, green and leatherback are the most threatened by the trade among marine turtles.

➤ Freshwater turtles endangered by the trade are *Kachuga spp.* and *Trionyx spp.*

➤ There is substantial illegal trade in freshwater turtles from U.P. and Bihar to West Bengal for local consumption and smuggling to Bangladesh from where they are sent to the Far East as legal exports.[25]

Turtle derivatives

➤ The shields of the hawksbill turtle (carey) which are brown with a yellow marbling are known as tortoiseshell. Sometimes green turtle shell is also used as tortoiseshell.

➤ Tortoiseshell is made into spectacle-frames, boxes, earrings. bangles, cigarette holders and pieces of art.

➤ Full hawksbill turtle carapaces are also stuffed and sold as souvenirs

Marine turtle shell identification

Hawksbill

Olive Ridley

Loggerhead

Leather Back

Green

along with shells of most other marine species. The shells are often lacquered and painted on.

➢ Turtle skin is used as leather for manufacture of belts, purses etc. This is the scaly area of the front flippers and is called 'a set' in the trade.

➢ Turtle shell is also used in the manufacture of traditional musical instruments.

Enforcement tips

➢ Marine turtles are poached in Orissa, West Bengal and Tamil Nadu while freshwater turtles are caught in most large river systems of the country. Egg-laying and hatching seasons of different species are the most important time for protection against poaching. This varies with each species.

➢ If you burn tortoiseshell it becomes a black lump and gives out a smell of burning hair. Imitations will char and give out a smell of burning plastic or milk. Also, under a microscope the dark areas of true tortoiseshell will appear as small dots of colour while in plastic the whole area will have a uniform colour.[2]

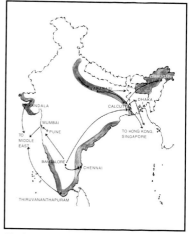

Turtle distributtion and trade routes

➢ Tests for refractive index and specific gravity are conclusive to distinguish tortoiseshell from imitations.[2]

Substance	Refractive index	Specific gravity
Tortoiseshell	1.55	1.29
Casein	1.53-1.54	1.32-1.34
Cellon	1.48	1.26
Rhodoid	1.48	1.28
Celluloid	1.49-1.50	1.38-1.42

Tortoiseshell comb for sale in Japan

Turtle shell scutes being exported to Sri Lanka

Frogs

- Frogs and toads are amphibians with a countrywide distribution.
- Frogs leg come mostly from the true frogs or family Ranidae, especially *Rana tigerina, Rana crassa* and *Rana hexadactyla,* which are protected under Schedule-IV of the Wildlife (Protection) Act.

Frogs legs

- Considered a luxury food in Europe (especially France and Belgium), East Asia (countries in Indo-China) and parts of India (Kerala, Tamil Nadu and Andhra Pradesh).
- Frogs are a natural pest control mechanism. The export of frozen frogs leg (FFL) has diminished the frog population and had a direct impact on the amount of chemical pesticides imported.
- More money was spent on import of chemical pesticides in those years than was earned through export of frogs leg.
- Total trade of FFL involved about 200 million Asian frogs per year.

Frogs leg exported to Belgium

- From India some 70 million frogs were exported in 1983.
- Frogs leg export from India is banned.
- The world trade is now supplied largely by legal exports from Indonesia and Bangladesh and illegally from India.

Enforcement tips

- Frogs leg leave the country mainly through the Indo-Bangladesh border in refrigerated trucks.
- They are normally labelled sea-food or chicken legs and may be concealed in those consignments.
- Frogs leg are also served in country-liquor and toddy shops along the coastal belt in Kerala. This is apart from speciality French restaurants in five-star hotels.
- Frogs are caught during the monsoon season in paddy fields or other places with shallow water. The legs are cut off on the spot or in small holding areas and then sold to the traders.
- A major destination for frogs leg is Brussels in Belgium which is the main processing centre.
  In India, the cities of Calcutta, Vishakapatanam and Kochi are major centres of the trade.

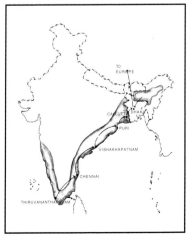

Trade routes of frogs leg

Edible-nest Swiftlet

> Globally, there are four swiftlet species whose nests are valued commercially.[26] Two of them are found in India: the edible-nest swiftlet (*Collocalia fuciphaga*) and the Indian edible-nest swiftlet (*Collocalia unicolor*).[27]

> Both species remain unprotected under Indian law, an apparent omission. The species was included in Appendix-II of CITES in 1997.

> Although no population estimate is available for the two swiftlets, one study estimates less than 2,000 breeding pairs in the Nicobars and notes that the species is "critically threatened."[27]

> Although technically nests can be collected after the bird finishes nesting, this is not practised in India and it seriously affects breeding success.[27]

Edible-nest of swiftlet

making soups), as a tonic (especially taken after a prolonged disease to recuperate) and as an aphrodisiac.[27]

> The Indian edible-nest swiftlet makes its nest with saliva mixed with grass and feathers. This is called 'black nest' by the trade. The edible-nest swiftlet of the Andaman and Nicobar islands makes its nest only from saliva. This is far more valuable and is known as 'white nest'.[27]

Swiftlet's nest

> Nearly 20 million swiftlets' nests enter the global trade annually.[1]

> Swiftlet's nests are used as food (for

Enforcement tips

> CITES considers the nest a biological derivative as it is made out of saliva.

> The nest collecting season begins in the Nicobars in the end of February, although collection in December and April-May is also known.[27]

> Thai boats illegally fishing in Indian waters are possible couriers of the nests. Seizures have taken place in Calcutta.[27]

> Nests which have been sun-dried after soaking (to remove unwanted matter) resemble fibres, but the ones that have been press-dried after soaking resemble glutinous plastic-like sheets with some fibres embedded.[27]

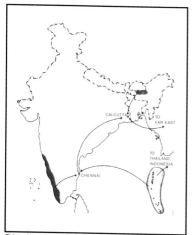

Distribution of swiftlets and trade route of nests

Live coral

➤ Corals are the skeletons of marine animals called polyps that accumulate over years to form large coral reefs.

➤ Coral reefs are the 'rainforests' of the sea, they provide a place for marine life to lay eggs, feed and hide, and create a physical barrier for coasts against destructive wave action.

Coral trade

➤ Corals are used as decorations in drawing rooms as well as cut and polished to make jewellery, jewellery boxes, vases, statues etc. They are also used in the pharmaceutical industry as a source for prostoglandins and terpenoids.[8]

➤ Corals are collected by underwater diving, by dredging the ocean floor using trawling nets, and by dynamiting parts of the coral reef. The last two methods cause untold damage to the underwater eco-system.

➤ Main trade categories of coral are stony corals (mostly *Fungia, Acropora, Pocillopora, Porites* generas), blue corals (*Heliopora*), fire corals (*Millepora*), Gorgonian corals (*Gorgonacea*) and black corals *(Antipathacea)*. While the first category yields most of the decorative corals, the others yield the semi-precious ornamentation corals. Gorgonian corals are especially sought after for the pharmaceutical trade.[28]

➤ The Philippines and Indonesia top the list of producer countries but coral from the Gulf of Mannar, the Gujarat coast and the Lakshadweep Islands are equally in demand and in danger.

➤ The cost of extracts that are refined and processed for commercial use is

Types of coral in trade

Corallium necklaces or jewellery

Antipatharia necklaces

Heliopora and Gorgonacea jewellery boxes

Ornamental corals (brain, fan and tree)[28]

Coral

Coral necklaces being sold in Japan; (inset)Coral and starfish souvenirs

50,000 times that of raw coral.[8]

➤ Coral skeletons are basically calcium carbonate that becomes calcium oxide or lime when heated. Corals are used to make commercial lime. Nearly two kg of coral is required to make one kg of lime.[29]

➤ Recent advances have made it possible for hobbyists to keep coral alive in their aquariums and this has caused a great increase in the demand for live coral.[29]

Enforcement tips

➤ Corals are often exported marked as shells which are rarely protected the world over.[28]

➤ Identification is often difficult as there are several look-alike species. Consult marine biologists for positive identification.

➤ Corals may be live or dead and this is equally difficult to determine for an amateur. Consult an expert.

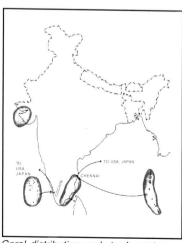

Coral distribution and trade routes

Butterflies and moths

➤ Butterflies and moths are lepidopterans that are present throughout the country. There are approximately 1,000 species of butterflies in India.

➤ Butterflies are important indicators of the health of an eco-system, more so than many mega-species.

➤ 234 species are protected by the Wildlife (Protection) Act, 1972 and two species are on CITES Appendix-II.

Butterflies and moths being smuggled in whisky cartons from Delhi

Trade in lepidopterans

➤ Butterflies and moths are traded as dead and live specimens. Dead specimens are mainly for collectors, for research and sometimes for exotic uses such as textile designing in Japan. Live ones are for butterfly houses.

➤ Of the millions of butterflies and moths that enter the trade, the most common is the swallow-tail family (out of the 500 species in the world more than 75 are endangered).[1] Some

families such as Papilionidae, Danidae, Lycaenidae etc are special targets of collectors in India.

➤ Birdwing butterflies or Ornithopterans are the largest of all butterflies and fetch the highest prices. All Ornithoptera are prohibited from international trade but are still smuggled.[1]

Enforcement hints

➤ Butterflies are largely collected in the Himalayas (both eastern and western).

➤ Collectors catch butterflies with nets, and moths with attraction devices such as lights, funnel traps with bait etc., in the night. This equipment cannot be easily concealed and tourists should be checked in sensitive areas.

➤ Many live butterflies enter the trade as pupa. They are then hatched in the country of import.

➤ The illegal butterfly trade is mainly carried out by mail and some by personal carriage. Butterflies in luggage are difficult to detect as the insects are put into envelopes with their wings folded, forming thin insertions.

➤ Some foreign tour operators advertise and operate butterfly catching expeditions in India.

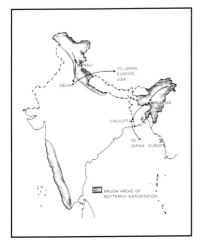

Major endemic butterfly areas and trade routes

Antlers

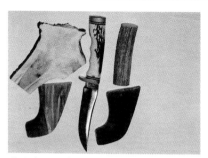

Cut pieces of antler for use as pistol and knife handles

Deer

➤ India has nine species of deer. Most deer species have antlers which are solid, branched structures, shed and re-grown every year. In this way they differ from horns of goats, cows and antelopes which are hollow, not branched and which are never shed.

➤ The antlers of chital (*Axis axis*), sambar (*Cervus unicolor*), swamp deer (*Cervus duvauceli*), barking deer (*Muntiacus muntjak*) and hog deer (*Axis porcinus*) are in the trade.[3]

➤ All deer species in India are protected.

Antlers

➤ 300 tons of shed antler products from Chital and Sambar were allowed to be exported from 4 major ports. This has been banned since April 1999 to promote conservation of deer species since shed antlers recycle nutrients.

➤ Antlers are used for manufacturing cutlery handles, pistol butts and buttons.[3]

➤ Used in Chinese and Tibetan medicine, mainly in the velvet stage, and as a powder in Ayurveda and Unani medicines.

Enforcement tips

➤ Antlers that are shed will always have a hollow socket while those removed from dead animals will have a section of the bony part of the skull attached to the burr. The latter may be from poached animals or from naturally dead animals. Very few of the latter reach the trade. (see Annexure-IV and V for identification techniques).

➤ Antlers in velvet are not shed and therefore the chances are that the animal has been poached.

➤ Misdeclaration of quantity and species have been revealed in the trade. Forgery of the legal procurement certificate (LPC) is also known.

➤ Cut and semi-processed pieces can be identified using forensic techniques.

➤ Uttar Pradesh, Madhya Pradesh, Maharashtra and Orissa are major illegal collection centres. Varanasi and Mughalsarai are important trade centres.

➤ Ayurveda uses powdered dry antler.

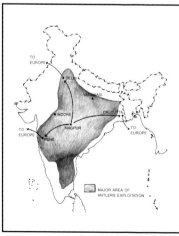

Antler trade routes

Kuth roots and pedicure product

Medicinal plants and roadside vendor

Medicinal plant species

➢ Of the 2,500 species of medicinal plants in India, 150 are used commercially and at least 2,000 in traditional medicines.

➢ Species such as rosy periwinkle (*Catharanthus roseus*), foxglove (*Digitalis spp*), quinine (*Cinchona ledgeriana*), costus or kuth (*Sassaurea costus*), rauwolfia root (*Rauvolfia serpentina*), Himalayan yew (*Taxus wallichiana*), yam (*Dioscorea deltoidea*), belladonna (*Atropa belladonna*), Himalayan mayapple (*Podophyllum hexandrum*), spikenard, Indian nard (*Nardostachys grandiflora*) are commercially traded in India.

➢ See Annexure-II for list of plants banned for export.

Trade in medicinal plants

➢ Four billion people rely on herbal medicines in the world. India is second only to Brazil in its supply.

➢ The major areas of collections in India are the Himalayas, North-Eastern India and the western ghats.

➢ The term 'artificially propagated' refers only to plants grown from seeds, cuttings, divisions, plant tissues or spores under controlled conditions. Controlled condition includes human intervention activities such as irrigation, fertilisation, weed control, nursery operations etc. Plants propagated without particular care in semi-natural conditions are not considered artificially propagated for CITES purposes. If the plant has a graft then both the graft and the root-stock must be artificially propogated to gain the exemptions given under that section.

➢ A wild collected plant grown in a nursery is a cultivated plant and not artificially propogated.

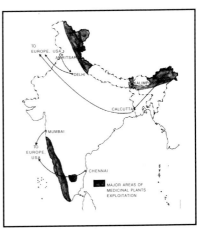

Medicinal plant trade routes

Medicinal plants

Enforcement hints

➤ For all plants being exported, a no objection certificate is needed, and they can be exported only from Bombay, Delhi, Calcutta, Madras and Kochi.

➤ A wild plant can get as much as three times the price of a cultivated one.

➤ Look at the leaves and roots of the plant if present (see illustration). Wild plants will have more pest marks on the leaves and their roots will be of varied shapes and sizes. Cultivated or artificially propagated plants will be more or less similar looking and in the case of the latter have less signs of pestilence.

➤ Check even medicines and beauty care products if possible. These could contain specified medicinal plants.

➤ Record exports species-wise and not as 'bulk drugs' or 'crude drugs'. Exporters of medicinal plants are required to state the scientific name and not merely the English or vernacular name, which varies from state to state.

➤ Encourage artificial propagation of medicinal plants among villagers as eco-development measures and ensure equitable distribution of profits to them.

➤ Check on supply of wild plants to established Indian pharmaceutical companies and Ayurveda doctors.

➤ In protected areas ensure that medicinal plants collection does not take place as part of minor forest produce collections.

Wild leaves   *Artificially propagated leaves*

Wild Roots   *Artificially propagated roots*

Ornamental plant species

- According to experts, one out of ten plant species in the world are endangered, rare or threatened.[1]
- Four families of plants that are in great demand as ornamental plants are orchids, cacti, insectivorous plants and cycads.
- Orchids such as *Paphiopedilium rothschildianum*, the rarest orchid in the world, can fetch whopping prices on the international market. From India, ladies slipper orchids such as *Paphiopedilium fairenium, P. villosum, P. venustom* etc are highly prized. So are the red and blue vandas (*Renanthera imschootiana* and *Vanda coerulea*) which are found in North-East India. Other Himalayan *Cypripedium* orchids are also in the trade.
- From India, cacti are least in demand internationally. There is a medium to large domestic demand for them.
- The rare southern Indian Beddome's cycad (*Cycas beddomei*) which is found only in one isolated pocket in Andhra Pradesh is the most endangered of the country's cycads.

Orchid in bloom

Cycads are a very primitive family of plants and are almost universally threatened by the trade.
- Of Indian insectivorous plants, the pitcher plant (*Nepenthes khasiana*) of North-Eastern Himalayas is the most common species in the trade. Internationally, plants such as the sundew plant, venus's fly trap and the bladderwort plant are in great demand.

Trade in ornamental plants

- The trade in ornamental plants may be to supply households with good looking plant species with showy or scented flowers or otherwise. It may also be for specialised plant collectors, botanical gardens and any establishment looking for unique plant species.
- Of the three million orchids that enter the global market annually, half are obtained from the wild.[1]
- Of the 10 million cactus plants in the global market every year, at least 300,000 are wild collected.

Enforcement hints

- Ornamental plants are often taken out as bulbs with a few leaves. If a large consignment, look for signs that will indicate that the plant is wild collected. Compared to wild collected plants, cultivated plants are more

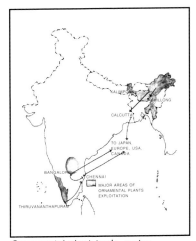
Ornamental plant trade routes

uniform in size and shape and will have fewer marks of pest damage on their leaves.

➢ Check LPC in case of suspicion by contacting issuing officer. This document is easily forged.

➢ Wild orchids are smuggled out mixed with cut flowers declared as lilies or other similar looking species.

Cactus plant in Sikkim

CITES regulations for plants

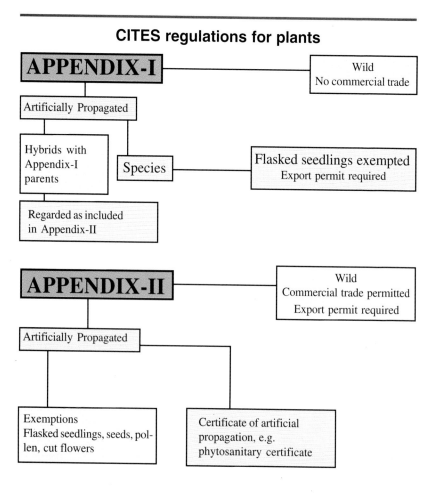

Timber Species

➤ The timber trade along with fisheries is the most difficult to monitor because of two reasons. Firstly, both provide mankind with essential resources unlike other wildlife trade. Secondly, both have a large number of traded species, making it very difficult to monitor.

➤ According to FAO, 41 species of tropical trees are endangered by the trade.[1]

➤ In the Himalayas species such as pine (*Pinus* spp), and deodar (*Cedrus deodara*) are highly prized. Timber slightly lower down in the terai such as sal (*Shorea robusta*) and shisham (*Dalbergia sissoo*) are targeted by the timber traders.

➤ In central India, sal and teak (*Tectona grandis*) mix along with species like tendu and koroi (*Albizzia* spp). The principal teak area of India is the trijunction of Madya Pradesh, Orissa and Maharashra. High quality teak also comes from Assam and Andaman Islands and Nilambur in Kerala.

➤ In north east India large, evergreen, pterocarps and dipterpcarps are predominant in the trade. An example of this is *toon*.

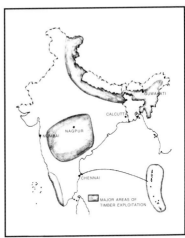

Timber trade routes

➤ The Himalayas and the central plateaus of India are the most affected by logging.

Enforcement hints

➤ A tree once cut is dead. Prevent cutting of trees more vigilantly than stopping the movement of cut logs.

➤ All export of logs, chips, barks. powder, flakes, dust, pulp or charcoal is banned in India.

➤ All timber movement in India requires transport permits (TPs) from the forest department. Check permits to see whether consignment is legal.

Trade in timber

➤ Illegal trade in timber is one of the most destructive of wildlife trades as it not only targets the species but also their habitat.

➤ It is estimated that globally more than 30 million acres of tropical forest are lost every year due to the timber trade. This is equal to about 50 acres every minute.[1]

➤ According to calculations, at the current rate, all the world's tropical forests outside protected areas will vanish in less than 80 years.[1]

Timber being transported in Assam

Trade in ornamental fish and molluscs

➤ Ornamental fish are the most popular pets in the USA (and parts of Europe) with 350-500 million fish being kept in USA alone. This is three times the number of dogs and cats combined.

➤ Estimates of the world trade are around 350 million fish per annum which is valued at US $ 600 million.

➤ Japan alone deals with at least 2000 species of fish in its domestic market. West Germany, Netherlands and UK are also large importers.

➤ Mortalities are very high in this trade with upto fifty percent of certain tropical fish (especially marine fish and invertebrates) dying during or just after capture and another ten to forty percent dying after transportation. Inexperienced keeping which leads to species incompatibility and poor water quality also results in high mortality. The volumes of fish caught to supply the trade are therefore phenomenal.

➤ Ornamental fish and molluscs are not protected under Indian law although the CITES Appendices do list some of the more commonly traded species.

➤ Shell fishing is very common in the Andaman and Nicobar Islands, in the Gulf of Mannar and a few other places along the coasts of India. The main methods used are diving and hand collecting, although at times nets, trawling and dynamiting coral reefs are used.

Species in trade

➤ Guppies (*Poecilidae*), mollies (*Cyprinodontidae*), swordtails (*Xiphophorus* spp.) and tetras (*Hyphessobrychon* spp) are some of the common tropical aquarium fish in the trade.

➤ The Asian boneytongue (*Sclerophagus formosus*) exemplifies the endangerment of a species by the ornamental trade and is listed on CITES Appendix I

➤ Among molluscan shells in India the Turban shell (*Turbo* spp.) and the top shell (*Trochus* spp) are the most endangered by the trade. Species like the holy chank, the scorpion shell, the king shell, the queen shell, cowries and windowpane oyster shells also figure in large quantities in the trade.

Enforcement hints

➤ Large number of consignments of ornamental fish enter and exit Calcutta, Madras and Bombay by air. The trade is mainly with the Far East especially to Bangkok and Singapore. Check even personal hand baggage for polythene bags filled with water and fish.

➤ Shells of molluscs can be traded in the form they are collected, after polishing and varnishing or in the form of handicraft.

Shell collected in the Andamans

Feathers

➢ Feathers, both shed and plucked from killed birds, are exported for decoration and use in handicrafts.

➢ The use of feathers in fishing floats is a large business. Those of the grey junglefowl (*Gallus sonneratii*), and the peacock pheasant (*Polyplectron bicalcaratum*) are particularly valuable.

➢ The orange-brown spotted neck feathers of the junglefowl are used as cheeks of a fishing fly and the green tail feathers of the peacock pheasant for body, wing, topping, tail or hackle (see illustration).

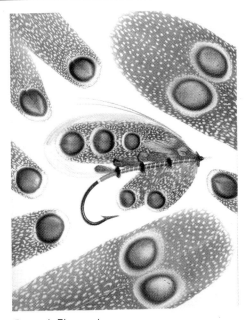

Peacock Pheasant

Grey Junglefowl

➢ Other species such as white- breasted kingfisher (*Halcyon smyrnensis*) are also used.

➢ Feathers are mostly smuggled through the postal system, or are hand carried.

➢ Feathers are smuggled mainly to Europe and North America. United Kingdom and Netherlands are known destinations.

Others

*T*rade in wildlife is diverse and enforcement officers will continually discover different species and derivatives being traded. As demand is variable, new species in trade or a new route can never be ruled out. Some species and derivatives traded in India that cannot be strictly categorised, are:

Shark Fins

➢ Fins of several shark species are commonly in the trade especially in the Far East and South East Asia.

➢ The fins are primarily used as a medicine in traditional oriental medicine (sold in shops in a dried form) or used in the culinary trade as an ingredient of the popular sharkfin soup.

Sharkfins for sale

➢ In India the main trade is from the Andaman & Nicobar Islands while the major trade centres are Port Blair & Calcutta.

➢ As shark meet is not a preferred meat and as prices are very low, fin gatherers often defin the shark and throw the remaining body overboard. The definned shark is left to die in the water. This is both a very cruel practice and is also a wasted resource in a fishing sense.

Hair and bristles

➢ The hair of the common mongoose (*Herpestes edwardsi*) and wild pig (*Sus scrofa*) and camel, horse and pig are used to make painting and shaving brushes.

➢ Pure wild hair brushes are rare, but command high prices in Europe and parts of North America and South-East Asia.

➢ Forensic examination can differentiate most species although confusion still exists between wild and domestic pigs.

➢ Shipments are made by parcel post or are hand carried.

Spiders

➢ There is a small trade in live spiders from the Himalayas and from south and east India to supply hobbyists and collectors in USA, Japan, Canada and Germany.

➢ Spiders most in demand are tarantulas, and other poisonous, brightly coloured species.

➢ Spiders are not protected in India. This needs to be rectified.

Horse-shoe crabs

➢ The horse-shoe crab is a marine invertebrate which is one of the oldest species in the world. It evolved many hundred million years ago.

➢ This primitive species come ashore in large numbers on certain nights and are collected on the beaches, or by fishing nets in the coast of eastern India, especially Orissa.

➢ The crabs have blue blood which is in great demand for medical research all over the world.

➢ These species are not protected in India.

*O*ne of the problems facing law enforcers today is the presence of a large number of confusing fakes in the trade. Artificial rhino horns and ivory, fake skins of tiger and leopard, fake musk pods and bear gall bladders are all known to be offered by traders. In some cases, such as, fake rhino horns and tiger parts, it has become a small-scale industry. It takes patience and skill to differentiate a fake from a genuine item. Five important rules are:

1. Always pre-suppose that the item could be a fake. Even if a fake, remember that it could involve the parts of another protected species.
2. Look for attempts to fake the original product. By careful observation, cut marks, colouring, shortening of hairs or other tell-tale marks can usually be seen.
3. Always book a person with fakes under the cheating law (Section 420 CrPc) or under any other relevant section to discourage this trade. It not only increases the demand for the actual commodity but also wastes a lot of valuable enforcement time.
4. A fake normally costs much less than the original item. This in itself should be a warning that it may not be genuine. In some cases, however, traders may pass off fakes at the same price as the original.
5. Adulteration is also common. For example, musk is often adulterated with bee's wax. Similarly, full elephant tusks have been discovered to be filled with cement to increase the sale weight. Although these are not traditionally used methods, they are practices that enforcement officers should be aware of.

Adulteration of musk

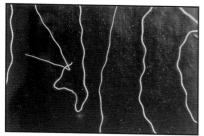

Genuine shahtoosh guard hair

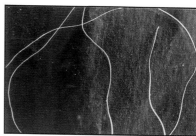

Pashmina guard hair

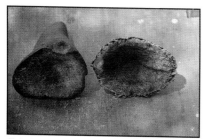

Fake(L) and real(R) rhino horn (underside)

Fake rhino horn made from buffalo horn

Tiger penises; fake (above & middle) and real (bottom)

Fake tiger skin made from dog skin

Buttons made of cow-horn, buffalo-horn and antlers (L to R)

Clockwise from top left : Musk extract, musk pod, fake pod, chemical musk

*W*ildlife agencies are forever having to handle live specimens of mammals, birds and reptiles for identification, disposal or other purposes. Handling reptiles is particularly dangerous as many of them are poisonous and others bite harder than the officer might imagine. The following precautions are necessary before attempting to handle reptiles.

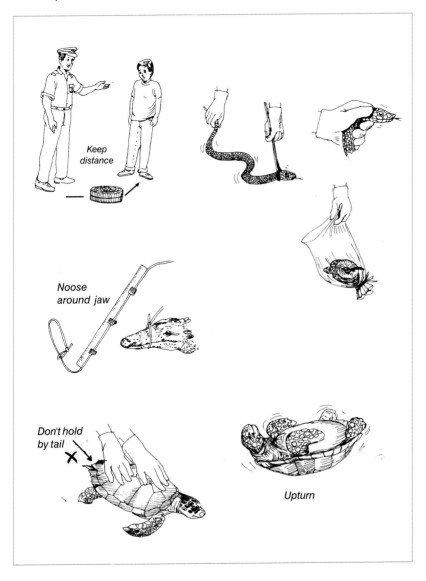

As per notification no. 2 (RE-98) 1997-2002 dated 13th April 1998 by the Ministry of Commerce, the export of following plants/plant portion and their derivatives and extracts obtained from the wild is prohibited.

1. Cycas beddomei (Beddome's cycad)
2. Vanda coerulea (Blue vanda)
3. Saussurea costus (Kuth or costus root)
4. Paphiopedilium species (Ladies slipper orchid)
5. Nepenthes khasiana (Pitcher plant)
6. Renanthera imschootiana (Red vanda)
7. Rauvolifia serpentina (Sarpagandha)
8. Ceropegia species
9. Frerea indica (Shindal Mankundi)
10. Podophyllum hexandrum (Indian Podophyllum)
11. Cyatheaceae species (Tree Ferns)
12. Cycadacea species (Cycads)
13. Dioscorea deltoidea (Elephant's Foot)
14. Euphorbia species (Euphorbias)
15. Orchidaceae species (Orchids)
16. Pterocarpus santalinus (Redsanders)
17. Taxus wallichiana (Common Yew or Birmi leaves)
18. Aquilaria malaccensis (Agarwood)
19. Aconitum species
20. Coptis teeta
21. Coscinium fenestrum (Calumba wood)
22. Dactylorhiza hatagirea (Hathjari)
23. Gentiana kurroo (Kuru Kutki)
24. Gnetum species
25. Kampheria galenga
26. Nardostachys grandiflora
27. Panax pseudoginseng
28. Picrorhiza kurrooa
29. Swertia chirata (Charayatah)

*T*he only conclusive test that distinguishes bear bile from bile of other animals, such as pigs and cattle which are often mixed in the trade, is the Thin Layer Chromatography test:

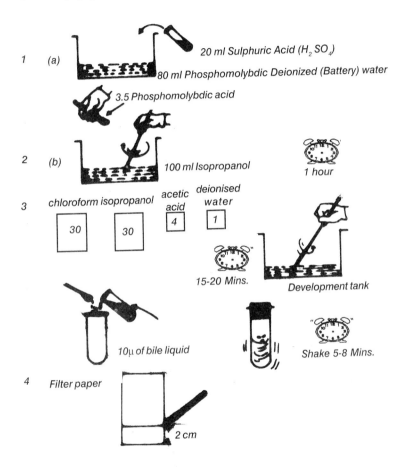

1   (a)   20 ml Sulphuric Acid (H_2SO_4)

80 ml Phosphomolybdic Deionized (Battery) water

3.5 Phosphomolybdic acid

2   (b)   100 ml Isopropanol   1 hour

3   chloroform   isopropanol   acetic acid   deionised water

| 30 | 30 | 4 | 1 |

15-20 Mins.   Development tank

10μ of bile liquid   Shake 5-8 Mins.

4   Filter paper   2 cm

Laboratory facilities for this test are available at the following institutions.

1. Wildlife Institute of India, Dehradun.
2. Indian Veternary Research Institute, Izat Nagar, Bareilly.
3. All Regional Forensic Laboratories.

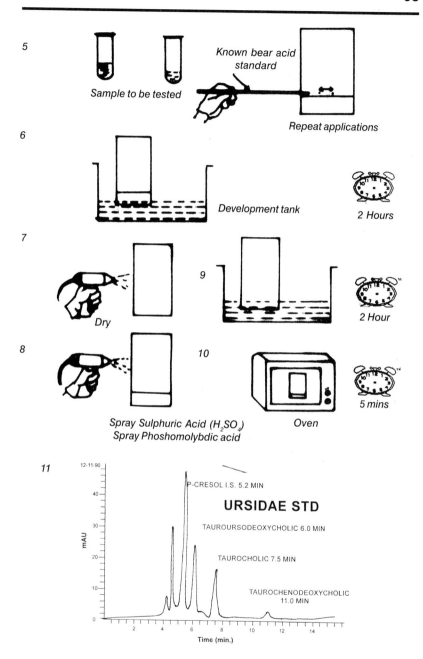

5 Sample to be tested Known bear acid standard Repeat applications

6 Development tank 2 Hours

7 Dry 9 2 Hour

8 10 Oven 5 mins

Spray Sulphuric Acid (H₂SO₄)
Spray Phoshomolybdic acid

11

12-11-90

P-CRESOL I.S. 5.2 MIN

URSIDAE STD

TAUROURSODEOXYCHOLIC 6.0 MIN

TAUROCHOLIC 7.5 MIN

TAUROCHENODEOXYCHOLIC
11.0 MIN

mAU

Time (min.)

*T*he following species of deer antlers are common in the trade and may be found looking as depicted below if the seizure is made just after collection. Even when in smaller pieces look for tell-tale marks that can make identification easier. Length, girth, number of tines, grain etc are pointers to identify antlers.

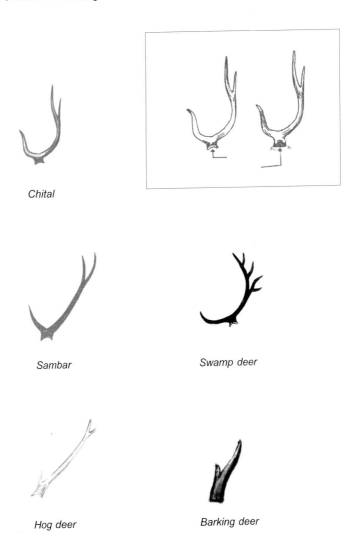

Chital

Sambar

Swamp deer

Hog deer

Barking deer

(Inset) Difference between shed antler(L) and cut antler(R)

*T*he illustrations below are of horns of Indian wild goats, antelope and cattle that may be found as trophies in trade. The horns may be separated from or still joined to the head of the specimen.

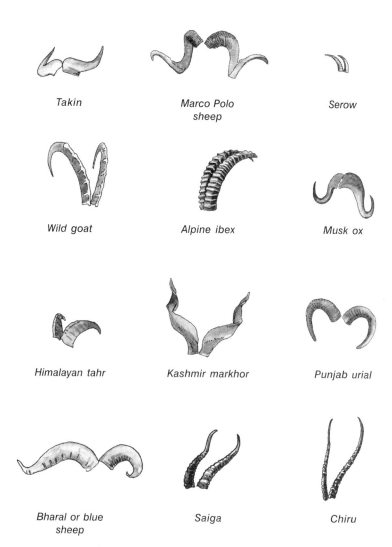

Takin	Marco Polo sheep	Serow
Wild goat	Alpine ibex	Musk ox
Himalayan tahr	Kashmir markhor	Punjab urial
Bharal or blue sheep	Saiga	Chiru

*A*lthough Asian elephant ivory is the most common ivory in trade in India, all the ivory illustrated below is in the world trade and may pass through India. There have been documented instances of trade in walrus and narwahl ivory in India in the past.

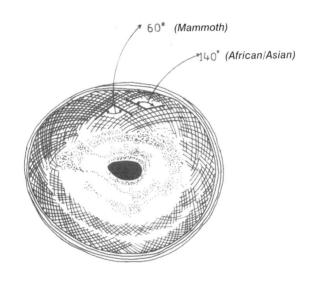

60° *(Mammoth)*

140° *(African/Asian)*

Schreger lines test for extinct and extant elephant ivory

Whole tusk

Cross section

*Narwahl
(Monodon monoceros)*

Whole teeth   *Cross section*

Killer whale (Orcinus orca)

Whole teeth   *Cross section*

Walrus (Odobenus rosmarus)

Whole teeth

Cross section   *Cross section*
Lower canine   *Incisor*

Hippopotamus (Hippopotamus amphibius) teeth

Annexure-VI : Eco message

*A*n eco-message is the preferred way for messages on wildlife crime to be transmitted to Interpol. This message can only be transmitted out of India by the Central Bureau of Investigation (CBI, Interpol unit) but can be filled in by other enforcement agencies and given to the CBI.

Subjects (Numbers and Items)	Clarification
1. Subject	Short description of the infraction.
Code name/Reference number	Possibly the name given to the operation.
Legal description of the offence	Legislation infringed and maximum and minimum penalties.
2. Place and method of discovery	Port of entry and address of discovery.
	Indicate how the offence was discovered (X-ray, documents examination, profile).
	If it is an autoroute, a waterway, in territorial waters or an airport, indicate position in nearest town and distance.
3. Date/time	If appropriate, specify period of infraction.
4. Species and description of the specimen (wildlife)	Common name of the species and a precise description of specimen (live, dead, part or derivative, age and sex is known). Quantity and estimated value. Specify units of measure and currency.
5. Identity of person(s) involved a) Family name (maiden name) b) First name(s) c) Sex d) Alias e) Date and place of birth f) Nationality g) Address h) Information contained in passport i) Profession j) Numbers of phone, fax, vehicles, companies etc. mentioned in 6. k) Other information	Number, place and date of issuance of the passport and ID. Period of validity. Items 5.a to 5.l must be filled in for each person involved in the infraction.
6. Companies Involved a) Type b) Name c) Activities d) Address and phone/fax	a) Indicate the legal type of company. b) Specify the official name and the usual trade name. c) Activities of the company. d) Address and phone/fax numbers of headquarter.

e) Registration number f) Business address and phone/fax	e) Registration number of the chamber of commerce. f) Business address and phone and fax Items 6.a to 6.e must be filled in for each person involved in the infraction.
7. Means of transportation and route	Provide the maximum amount of details on the means of transportation used and route.
8. a) Country and town of origin	Place of production of the waste. For CITES specimen, indicate country of origin according to CITES definition (Country where animal or the plant has been taken in the wild, bred in captivity or artificially propagated), country of origin according to Customs definition (Country where the last substantial transformation occurred). In case of specimens originated from the sea, indicate "sea".
b) Country of provenance	For CITES specimen country of last re-export.
c) Country(ies) of transit	Specify the country of transit declared on the transport documents.
d) Country and town of destination	Specify the destination declared on the transport documents and the real destination.
9 Identification of documents used	Specify the type of documents, including authorizations, transport documents, permits, invoices, reports of analysis, etc. Specify if documents are false, falsified or invalid.
10. Law enforcement agency	Specify the name and exact location of the agency (Address/telephone/fax numbers).
11. Modus operandi.	Describe precisely the modus operandi, including : a) Technique of dissemination, type of packaging used. b) Technique of falsification of financial statement of the involved companies, illicit transaction, possible relationship with other cases. c) Attach photocopies of the documents (e.g. false document) or photos.
12. Additional information	Other details deemed relevant.
13. Information requested	Do investigators need information detained by foreign countries?

*I*t is important to be able to quickly contact the agency or individual, most crucial for your enforcement work. The following list of addresses are the most important ones for enforcement in India.

- Chief Conservator of Forests & Chief Wildlife Warden Government of Andhra Pradesh, Aranya Bhawan, Saifabad, Hyderabad - 500 004. (A P) Tel : 040-24600272, 24650145 addlpccf_wl@efs.ap.gov.in

- Chief Wildlife Warden, Govt. of Andaman & Nicobar Islands, Vansadan, Haddo, Port Blair, South Andaman-744102 Tel : 03192-233270 Fax: 03192-230113

- Chief Conservator of Forests (Wildlife) Government of Assam, R. G. Baruah Road, Rehabari, Guwahati - 781 008 (Assam) Tel : 0361-2517064 Fax: 0361-2601425/2547386 pccf@onlysmart.com

- Chief Conservator of Forests (WL)-cum-Chief Wildlife Warden Government of Arunachal Pradesh, Itanagar - 791 111 (Arunachal Pradesh) Tel : 0360-2212243, 2204020,2212006

- Chief Conservator of Forests - cum Chief Wildlife Warden, Government of Bihar, 4th Manzhil, Vishweshraiah Technical Bhawan,Beli Road, Patna (Bihar) Tel & Fax : 0612- 2262544

- Additional Principal Chief Conservator of Forests & Chief Wildlife Warden, Government of Chhattisgarh, Jail Road, Raipur, (Chhattisgarh) Tel : 0771-331135, 331136 Fax : 0771-331135

- Chief Conservator of Forests (WL) -cum-Chief Wildlife Warden, Government of Gujarat, Dr. Jivraj Mehta Bhavan, Block No. 14, 1st Floor, Old Sachivalaya, Gandhinagar - 382 010, (Gujarat) Tel : 230007 Fax : 0712-221097 ccf_cwlw@gujarat.gov.in

- Addl. Prl.Chief Conservator of Forests (WL)-cum-Chief Wildlife Warden, Talland, Shimla-171 001 (Himachal Pradesh) Tel : 0177-2624193 Fax : 0177-2624193 forprojs@sancharnet.in

- Chief Wildlife Warden,
  Government of Jammu & Kashmir
  Tourist Reception Centre,
  Srinagar
  (Jammu & Kashmir)
  Tel : 0194-2476261
  Fax : 0194-2452469
  Fax : 0191-2544575

- Chief Conservator of Forests-cum-
  Chief Wildlife Warden,
  Government of Jharkhand,
  P.O. Hinoo, Ranchi (Jharkhand)
  Tel : 0651-2480655
  Fax : 0651-2480655
  ccf_wl@yahoo.co.in

- Prl. Chief Conservator of Forests
  (WL) & Chief Wildlife Warden,
  Karnataka State,
  Aranaya Bhawan, II Floor,
  18-Cross Road, Malleswaram,
  Bangalore - 560 003 (Karnataka)
  Tel : 080-23345846
  Fax : 080 23346389
  pccfwl@vsnl.com, pccffwl@eth.net

- Chief Conservator of Forests
  (WL) & Chief Wildlife Warden,
  Government of Kerala,
  Forest Headquarters,
  Vazhuthacaud,
  Thiruvananthapuram-695 014
  (Kerala)
  Tel & Fax : 0471-2322217

- Chief Conservator of Forests (WL),
  Chief Wildlife Warden,
  Government of Manipur,
  P.O. Sanjenthong,
  Imphal - 795 001 (Manipur)
  Tel : 03852-2223662
  Fax : 03852-2220394

- Chief Wildlife Warden,
  Government of Meghalaya,
  Lower Laichumiere, Risa Colony,
  Shillong - 793 001 (Meghalaya)
  Tel : 0364-227762
  Fax : 0364-228334

- Pl. Chief Conservator of Forests
  (WL) & Chief Wildlife Warden
  Government of Madhya Pradesh,
  Van Bhavan, Tulsi Nagar,
  Bhopal - 462 003
  (Madhya Pradesh)
  Tel : 0755-2557371, 2766315
  Fax : 0755-2766315
  pccfwl@sancharnet.in

- Chief Conservator of Forests
  (WL) & Chief Wildlife Warden,
  Government of Maharashtra State,
  Dr. Baba Saheb Ambedkar
  Bhawan,
  4 & 5th Floor, M.E.C.L. Building
  Seminary Hills Campus,
  Nagpur-440 006 (Maharashtra)
  Tel : 0712-2510758
  Fax : 0712-2510671

- Chief Wildlife Warden,
  Government of Mizoram
  Environment & Forest
  Department,
  Tuikhuahtlang,
  AIZAWL (Mizoram)
  Tel : 0389-325371
  cwlwmizoram@hotmail.com

- Chief Wildlife Warden,
  Government of Nagaland,
  DIMAPUR (Nagaland)
  Tel : 03862-226681
  Fax : 03662-226681

- Principal Chief Conservator of
  Forests (WL) & Chief Wildlife
  Warden,
  Government of Orissa,
  Prakriti Bhavan, 5th Floor,
  Government (BDA) Apartment
  Nilkantha Nagar, Nayapalli,
  BHUBANESWAR - 751 012
  (Orissa)
  Tel : 0674-2564587

- Chief Conservator of Forests (WL)
  Government of Punjab,
  SCO No. 2463-64,
  Sector No. 22-C
  CHANDIGARH (Punjab)
  Tel : 0172-2705828
  Fax: 0172-2705828

- Addl. Chief Conservator of Forests
  (WL) & Chief Wildlife Warden,
  Government of Rajasthan,
  Van Bhavan, Vaniki Path,
  JAIPUR - 302 005 (Rajasthan)
  Tel : 0141-2227832
  Fax : 0141-2227832

- Addl. Chief Conservator of
  Forests & Chief Wildlife Warden,
  Wildlife Circle,
  Government of Sikkim,
  Forest Secretariat,
  Deorali, Gangtok (Sikkim)
  Tel : 03592-22330
  Fax : 03592-22978, 26368

- Chief Wildlife Warden,
  Government of Tripura,
  Aranya Bhawan, Nehru
  Complex,
  P.O. Kunjaban,
  AGARTALA - 799 001,
  Tripura (West)
  Tel : 225223 Fax : 225253

- Principal Chief Conservator of
  Forests & Chief Wildlife Warden,
  Government of Tamilnadu,
  6D, Panagal Building,
  No 1, Jeenis Road, Saidapet,
  CHENNAI - 600 015 (Tamilnadu)
  Tel : 24321738 Fax : 24321884

- Chief Conservator of Forests &
  Chief Wildlife Warden,
  Government of Uttar Pradesh,
  17, Rana Pratap Marg,
  LUCKNOW (Uttar Pradesh)
  Tel : 2206584 Fax : 2222061

- Principal Chief Conservator of
  Forests (WL& Biodiversity) &
  Chief Wildlife Warden,
  Government of West Bengal,
  Bikas Bhawan, North Block, 3rd
  Floor, Salt Lake,
  Kolkata-700 091 (W.B.)
  Tel : 033-23345946, 23346900,
     23583208

- Conservator of Forests &
  Chief Wildlife Warden,
  Government of Goa,
  Junta House, 3rd Floor,
  PANAJI - 403 001 (Goa)
  Tel : 2224747, 2312095

- Conservator of Forests &
  Chief Wildlife Warden,
  Daman & Diu / Dadra & Nagar
  Haveli, Silwassa, DAMAN
  Tel & Fax : 0260-640283

- Director Animal Husbandry-cum-
  Chief Wildlife Warden
  Government of Pondicherry
  (PONDICHERRY)
  Tel : 0413-2349304, 2336088
  drdevarajifs@hotmail.com

- Chief Wildlife Warden,
  Daman & Diu, DAMAN
  Fax: 02636-32685/34922/34775

- Chief Conservator of Forests,
  Wild Life Wing, Govt. of Haryana,
  Forest Department,
  Van Bhawan,
  Forest Complex-C-18, Sector-6,
  PANCHKULA - 134 109
  (Haryana)
  Tel : 0172-2563988, 2584115

- Deputy Conservator of Forests
  Deptt. of Forest and Wildlife
  Govt. of NCT of Delhi,
  A-Block, 2nd Floor,
  Vikas Bhavan, I.T.O.
  New Delhi-110 007
  Tel : 22923561, 2297650

- Chief Conservator of Forests (WL)
  & Chief Wildlife Warden
  Govt. of Uttaranchal,
  87-Rajpur Road,
  DEHRA DUN - (Uttaranchal)
  Tel/Fax : 0135-2744225

- Administrator
  Govt. of Lakshadweep
  Kavaratti, Via Calicut-682 555

- Chief Wild Life Warden
  Estate Office, Union Territory
  Sector 17, Chandigarh

- Regional Deputy Director (ER)
  Nizam Palace, 234 / 4, AJC Bose
  Road,
  2nd MSO Bldg., Calcutta-700 020
  Tel : 033-247869 Fax : 2478698

- Regional Deputy Director (WR)
  11, Air Cargo Complex
  Sahar, Mumbai-400 099
  Tel : 022-8230666 Fax : 8230666

- Regional Deputy Director (WR)
  C-2A, Rajaji Bhawan, Besant
  Nagar, CGO Complex,
  Chennai-600 090
  Tel : 044-4916747

- Regional Deputy Director (NR)
  Bikaner House Barracks,
  Shahjahan Road,
  New Delhi-110 011
  Tel : 011-3384556

- Director
  Zoological Survey of India
  Ministry of Environment and
  Forests
  Government of India
  Nizam Palace, CGO Complex,
  14th Floor
  234/4, A.J.C. Bose Road,
  Calcutta-700 020
  Tel : 033-2478219, 033-2475463

- Director,
  Botanical Survey of India
  Brabourne Road,
  Calcutta-700 001
  Tel : 033-2424922

- Director
  Wildlife Institute of India,
  Post Box No. 18, Chandrabani,
  Dehradun-248 001
  Tel : 0135-2640112-115
  Fax : 0135-2640117
  wii.isnet@axcess.net.in

- Vice President &
  Executive Director,
  Wildlife Protection Society of India,
  M-52, Greater Kailash Part-I
  New Delhi-110 048
  Tel : 011-26294962
  Fax : 011-26464918
  wpsi@vsnl.com

- Director
  TRAFFIC-India
  WWF-India
  172-B. Lodi Estate,
  New Delhi-110003
  Tel : 011-24698578

1. Fitzgerald, S (1989) International Wildlife Trade, Whose Business is it?, WWF-USA.
2. Adapted from CITES information sheet, CITES Secretariat.
3. Menon.V et.al (1994), Wildlife Trade: A Handbook for Enforcement staff, TRAFFIC-India, WWF-India.
4. Adapted from Anon (1992): Asian Wildlife: Law Enforcement Workshop. US Fish and Wildlife Service Lecture Notes.
5. Adapted from notes by Pradeep Srivastava, DC, Delhi Police.
6. Adapted from manual on post-mortem techniques, Wildlife Institute of India.
7. Anon (1997)Proceedings of the CAMP Workshop for Indian Mammals
8. P.Kannan pers.comm.
9. Mills, J.A and C.Serveehn (1991), Asian Trade in Bear and Bear Parts, TRAFFIC-USA, WWF-USA
10. Green, M, Phd Thesis on musk deer, Cambridge Unversity.
11. V.G.Gogate pers.comm.
12. Seth S.D et.al (1975) Pharmacodynamics of Musk, Central Council for Research in Indian Medicine and Homeopathy, New Delhi
13. Sukumar ,R (1989) The Asian Elephant, Cambridge University Press
14. Menon,V, Sukumar,R and Kumar,A (1997), A God in Distress, Asian Elephant Conservation Centre and Wildlife Protection Society of India
15. Espinoza,E.O and Mann,M (1991) Identification Guide to Ivory and Ivory Substitutes
16. Menon,V (1996), Under Seige: Poaching and Protection of Greater One-horned Rhinoceroses in India, TRAFFIC-International, UK
17. Martin, E.B (1989) Report on the trade in rhino products in eastern Asian and India, Pachyderm
18. E.B. Martin, pers. comm.
19. Wright, B. (1998) India's Tiger Poaching Crisis, Wildlife Protection Society of India, New Delhi.
20. Read, B.E (1982) Chinese Materia Medica, Animal Drugs, Chinese Medicine Series(4), Southern Material Center, Inc, Taipei
21. Wright, B & Kumar, A (1997) Fashioned for Extinction, An Expose of the Shahtoosh Trade, Wildlife Protection Society of India
22. Gruisen J.V. & Sinclair, T. (1992), Fur Trade in Kathmandu, Implications for India, TRAFFIC-India, WWF-India.
23. Goyal, S.P (1998) Shahtoosh identification sheet, unpublished, Wildlife Institute of India
24. Ahmed, A. (1997), Live Bird Trade in Northern India, TRAFFIC-India, WWF-India.
25. Choudhury, B.C. & Bhupathy, S. (1993), Turtle Trade In India, A Study of Tortoises and Freshwater Turtles, TRAFFIC-India, WWF-India.
26. Lau,A.S.M & Melville,S (1994) International trade in swiftlets nest with special reference to Hong Kong, TRAFFIC-International.
27. Sankaran,R (1995) Impact assessment of nest collection on the edible-nest swiftlet in the Nicobar Islands, SACON.
28. Coffey, M (1991), A Guide to India and Pacific Corals common in the Wildlife Trade, US Fish and Wildlife Service, Division of Law Enforcement.
29. Bentley, N (1998) An overview of the Exploitation Trade and Manage-ment of Corals in Indonesia, TRAFFIC Bulletin Vol 17, No 2
30. Import-Export Policy, DGFT, GOI
31. Is it Really From a Bear? WSPA document.

Photo credits

Asian Elephant Conservation Centre
Page 57 (right).

Belinda Wright
Pages 3, 61 (top and bottom), 64,
65 (top right & left), 94 (second row
right and third row right).

Brij Bhushan Sharma
Pages 84, 94 (bottom row left).

Esmond Bradley Martin
Page 59 (left).

Fahmeeda Hanfee
Page 83 (bottom).

George Schaller
Page 67 (right).

Kathleen Conforti
Page 65 (bottom left)

Ravi Agarwal/Srishti
Pages 65 (middle right, bottom
right), 66 (all photos).

Stanley Breeden
Pages 55, 74.

Sukumar R
Pages 57(left), 59.

Vivek Menon
Pages 56, 62, 65 (top left), 67
(left), 69 top, 72 (top and
bottom),73, 75 (top),77, 78, 82 (top
and bottom), 83, 85, 87, 88, 92, 94
(second row left, third row left,
bottom row right).

Will Luiijf
Pages 75 (bottom), 79.

Wildlife Institute of India
Pages 63, 94 (top right and left).

Wildlife Protection Society of India:
Pages 54, 65 (middle left).

World Wildlife Fund-USA
Page 60 (right).

WILDLIFE PROTECTION SOCIETY OF INDIA

THE WILDLIFE PROTECTION SOCIETY OF INDIA (WPSI) was formed in 1994 with the specific aim of providing additional support and information to combat the escalating illegal wildlife trade.

The Society has established a network of informers throughout India, a comprehensive database on wildlife crimes, and a legal cell which pursues the prosecution of important wildlife cases, particularly those concerning the tiger.

WPSI assists and liaises with Government enforcement authorities to bring about the arrest of offenders ans seizure of wildlife products. With field projects and awareness campaigns, WPSI is actively involved in major wildlife conservation issues in India.